effortless entertaining cookbook

effortless entertaining cookbook

80 recipes that will impress your guests without stress

meredith steele

founder of the blog SteeleHouseKitchen.com (formerly InSockMonkeySlippers.com)

PAGE STREET
PUBLISHING CO.

PAGE STREET
PUBLISHING CO.

First published in 2016 by
Page Street Publishing Co.
27 Congress Street, Suite 103
Salem, MA 01970
www.pagestreetpublishing.com

Distributed by Macmillan, sales in Canada by The Canadian Manda Group.

19   18   17   16   1   2   3   4   5

ISBN-13: 9781624142642
ISBN-10: 1624142648

Library of Congress Control Number: 2016934741

Cover and book design by Page Street Publishing Co.
Photography by Meredith Steele

Printed and bound in China

Page Street is proud to be a member of 1% for the Planet. Members donate one percent of their sales to one or more of the over 1,500 environmental and sustainability charities across the globe who participate in this program.

Without the constant love and support of my parents, the laughter of my daughter, my husband's mad wine skills and our friends who always give me a great excuse to throw a party, this book would never have happened—thank you.

Introduction   10
A Very Good Time Indeed   12

spring   15

Let's Brunch   17
  Jamón Serrano Manchego Wraps with Quince Paste   18
  Black Pepper-Balsamic Strawberries   21
  Asparagus, Green Onion and Feta Frittata   22
  Overnight Croissant French Toast Bake with Coffee Rum Sauce   25
Easter Lunch   27
  Herbed Feta Dip   28
  Chive Deviled Eggs   31
  Shaved Asparagus Salad   32
  Rosemary Garlic Roasted Pork Loin with Fingerling Potatoes   35
  Orange Cardamom Cookies   36
Sunset Garden Party   39
  Bee's Knees Cocktail with Thyme Honey   40
  Chilled Shrimp with Cilantro Crème Fraîche   43
  Fava Bean and Cucumber Salad   44
  Apricot Curry Chicken Sandwiches   47
  Lemon Elderflower Icebox Cakes   48
Dinner with Friends   51
  Coconut Curry Mussels   52
  Carrot Ginger Soup with Mint Cashew Pesto   55
  Roasted Chicken with Fennel and Leek Croutons   56
  Chardonnay Poached Apricots   59

summer   61

Backyard Seafood Boil   63
  IPA Quick-Pickle Green Beans   64
  Fennel Bread   67
  Seafood Boil   68
  Sorbet and Prosecco   71

Fiesta Taco Bar   73
  Smoked Sea Salt Mescal Margaritas   74
  Oven Elotes   77
  Quick-Pickled Onion   78
  Tomatillo and Avocado Salsa   81
  Beer-Braised Carnitas   82
  Mango Granita with Honeyed Buttermilk   85
Summer Soirée   87
  Chorizo Gougéres   88
  Gazpacho with Lobster Relish   91
  10-Minute Garlic and Rosemary Roasted Salmon   92
  Sautéed Green Beans with Miso-Mustard Vinaigrette   95
  Vanilla Bean and Bourbon Peaches   96
Indian Summer Cookout   99
  Blistered Shisito Peppers with Sea Salt and Fish Sauce   100
  Heirloom Tomatoes and Burrata   103
  Grilled Flat Iron with Pineapple-Avocado Salsa   104
  Chipotle Roasted Potatoes   107
  No-Churn Caramelized White Chocolate Ice Cream   108

fall

Farmers' Market Brunch   113
  Persimmon Honeyed Yogurt with Toasted Hazelnuts   114
  Dutch Baby with Chai Caramel Pears   117
  Greens, Bacon and Eggs   118
  Toast with Sage Butter   121
Autumn Beer Dinner   123
  Speck and Mozzarella Crostini with Truffle Oil   124
  Bratwurst and Cabbage with Dunkel Sauce   127
  Slow-Cooker Mashed Potatoes   128
  Vanilla Panna Cotta with Blackstrap Molasses and Graham Crackers   131
Thanksgiving with Friends   133
  Bourbon Amaretto Cooler   134
  Dried Cherry and Sage Goat Cheese   137
  Shredded Kale and Brussels Sprout Salad   138
  Apple and Sausage Stuffing   141
  White Wine Braised Turkey Legs   142
  Pumpkin Pot de Crème with Maple Bourbon Whipped Cream   145

Game Day for Food Snobs 147

Curried Snack Mix 148

Porter-Braised Short Rib Nachos 151

Brown Sugar and Chipotle Wings 152

Caramelized Onion Dip 155

Whisky Caramel Brownies 156

winter 159

Wine and Dine 161

Bacon-Wrapped Dates with Rosemary Goat Cheese 162

Chilled Butternut Squash Salad with Roasted Shallot Dressing 165

Red Wine Braised Leg of Lamb 166

Make-Ahead Parmesan Risotto 169

Blue Cheese and Honey 170

Winter Harvest 173

Mushroom and Pancetta Tart 174

Orange and Olive Salad 177

Easy Duck Confit with Orange Honey Glaze 178

Roasted Cauliflower and Pomegranate Farro 181

Pumpkin Seed Brittle 182

The Big Holiday Gathering 185

Winter Pimm's Punch 186

Garlic and Rosemary Baked Camembert 189

Brown Sugar Glazed Ham 190

Creamed Parmesan Collard Greens 193

Smoked Paprika and Maple Carrots 194

Bourbon Pecan Pie Shortbread 197

Cocktails and Conversation 199

Champagne Bar 201

Cheese and Charcuterie Board 203

Marinated Olives 204

Roasted Fingerling Potatoes with Caviar and Smoked Salmon 207

Cardamom and Rose Water Tea Cookies 208

Orange Scented Palmiers 211

Resources 212

Acknowledgments 213

About the Author 214

Index 215

introduction

Sweet smells of blueberry muffins baking fill the kitchen, and the sounds of the morning soap operas' sordid affairs ring in my ears as I'm snapping beans. This is where my love of cooking all began—growing up in the kitchen with RoRo, my nanny. From collard greens to fried apricot pies, there was love and art in every dust of flour and stir of the pot and I always felt we were the only two that understood that. That passion for cooking and creating is shared by many, and, for some of us, that is how we show our love.

I've been cooking for as long as I can remember. Both of my parents worked and when my father died and my mother had to work even longer hours to keep us going, it was either cook or succumb to the fate of a Hungry Man Dinner.

As a teenager, I had subscriptions to *Gourmet, Living* and *Bon Appétit*—not what you would usually expect from a fourteen-year-old. I was enthralled by the photography and ideas of grand parties, but instead of dreaming to be a chef, I wanted to be a graphic designer so I could create what I saw in the magazines. When it came time to go to college, I headed off to art school and immersed myself in communication design, marketing and photography. I worked at a few advertising agencies and small publications for a number of years as a designer and art director; then, when it came time to have a child, my world drastically and dramatically changed.

She came into the world on a cool October morning under a nearly full moon. She was 16 weeks early, weighed a little over a pound and was fighting for every breath. I knew everything would be different the moment I heard the helicopter take her away to a critical care hospital. In that moment, I left my career and never looked back. I was now a mom desperately fighting for a child that had a seven percent chance of making it through the night.

Fast forward a year, and my days were suddenly full of dirty diapers, mountains of laundry and trying to feed a perfectly healthy and precocious baby girl. However, I hadn't given up my dreams of getting into something of my own, away from motherhood. I started a blog (called In Sock Monkey Slippers at the time), publishing organic baby food recipes, and it wasn't long before I had my first freelance job photographing baby food products for packaging. It was like being back at work again, but on my own terms, and I quickly realized I could actually balance being a mother and this type of work.

Now, many years later, I have my own recipe development and food photography business called MBS Recipe Development, still have a blog (now called Steele House Kitchen) and juggle photoshoots and meetings in between carpooling and soccer games. I have worked for everyone imaginable from large corporations to small publications, my work has been featured in national magazines, my blog was a finalist for the *Saveur* magazine Blog Awards and I've even worked for Jamie Oliver as a contributor for his website; I've become a firm believer that everyone has a path to something great no matter how long and winding that path may be.

This leads me to why I am writing this book. As mentioned earlier, I show love by cooking. If you receive an invite to my house for anything from a simple "come-on-over" dinner to an extravagant party, this is why. (Oh, and because I really like to throw parties.) It helps that my husband is a sommelier with years of restaurant experience under his belt and a recent move into wine sales. When you combine the two of us, we're an entertaining force to be reckoned with, and we can guarantee that a good time will be had by all.

I would love to invite you all over, but since that is not logistically possible, I hope you enjoy these simple pages filled with my recipes, a few cooking hacks, drink pairings and tips and tricks for a fabulous party that everyone can enjoy, including you—the host.

a very good time indeed

They say that the dinner party is dead, but I don't believe that for one second—for what's more enjoyable than sitting around somewhere comfortable with good food and drinks with favorite friends? Maybe we've just simply forgotten the joy of it all—or that just a little effort can create wonderful and memorable events in our own homes. My ideal gathering is a comfortable and inspiring one; it doesn't matter if we're all dressed to the nines or kicking back in flip flops, we should all be having a good time!

The intention of this book is to create a collection of recipes that reflect my penchant for creative cuisine but are basic enough that you are not hovering over the stove and can enjoy the party too. The recipes are arranged by seasonal menus and gathered together so the flavors flow from one meal to the next. There are also plenty of wine and beer pairings so you're not stuck at a store staring cluelessly at a wall of wine with a tinge of panic.

I like to think of this book as a casual guide for events that come in all shapes and sizes—game day to holiday—and are unique enough to set you apart from the crowd. Whether you use these menus in their entirety or are just inspired by a few recipes to help you pull together your own menu, I hope this cookbook leaves you inspired enough to open your doors to those you love to spend time with.

To get started, here are a few reliable tips for a successful, stress-free party:

be a planner

Send out invites, whether as traditional as a card in the mail or as casual as an e-vite or a phone call, at least two weeks in advance. When planning your guest list, invite people you know have similar interests or you know will flow well together. At the same time that you send out invitations, start planning your menu.

prep like a boss

Prepare and prepare again. Fill your menu mostly with recipes you can make or mostly prepare in advance. While cooking, clean as you go and always start with an empty dishwasher before guests arrive. Not only should you prep your food, but prepare your table the day before. Whether it's a sit down meal or a buffet, having seats and place settings done in advance can help tremendously. I even go as far as to set out serving dishes with post-it notes to remind me what goes in each one. It doesn't matter if you've gone so far as to have full place settings or disposable tableware; prepare as much as you can ahead of time. All that planning and cooking in advance is completely worth it if all you have to do is lay out food and turn on some music when the party starts.

the hospitable host

The secret to a great dinner party is making your guests feel comfortable. From the moment they arrive, offer a beverage or guide them to an area where you have created a self-serve bar and some light hors d'oeuvres. Even if your party is as casual as can be, the first thing you should offer is to come in and feel at home, and always keep glasses and bellies full.

it's all in the details

The little details can make a night truly memorable. Background music is a must and a good playlist to set the mood of the party is essential. Fresh seasonal flowers and unscented candles can also play a big role in making guests feel relaxed and pampered. Winter events call for a fire in the fireplace or outdoor firepit for extra ambience. Then there are the responsible details, like hiring a babysitter if children are around and making sure your rideshare app or a taxi service is on standby. All of this shows you know what you're doing and you're telling your guests "I've got this; it's going to be a good time."

now enjoy

You wouldn't have put this together if you didn't love to cook and entertain. You have prepped and prepped again, and all you can do now is have fun! Sit back, relax and pour a glass of wine before everyone arrives. Most importantly, remember, if something goes wrong—like your grill burns your meal to a crisp—there's always delivery and everyone loves a good party story. You have no idea how many times I've left the lid to the cocktail shaker loose and made an insane mess. It is what it is, and you just have to roll with it. Your guests are here because they enjoy your company no matter what happens!

spring

When the tulip tree and red bud in our backyard break their silence and explode in pink blankets of flowers, I know it's time to dust off our patio and get ready for a party. Spring is the time of year I really start to entertain. I spend most of my time in the garden trying to get herbs resettled and summer tomatoes in the ground and after a long day, all I want to do is celebrate the good weather. From Easter egg hunts to toasting the sunset with friends, spring parties are a good taste of what's to come for the rest of the year.

brunch

jamon serrano manchego wraps
with quince paste

black pepper
balsamic strawberries

asparagus, green onion,
and feta frittata

croissant french toast
with coffee rum sauce

let's brunch

I'm always looking for a reason to have a party and the transformation of nature shedding its cold winter brown coat for a fresh green spring one is certainly cause for celebration. Once the sun starts to shine a little brighter, our patio is always full on the weekends, especially for brunch—when we open the windows, turn on some music and watch the kids play in the backyard while we're all lounging around with the sun hitting our faces.

Brunch is usually a very casual affair for us and is not always planned days in advance. It's all about relaxing and enjoying the day with everyone, so I like to put out large platters of food and a stack of plates and utensils on a gorgeous table full of spring flowers and let everyone help themselves as they please. Of course you can't have a brunch without champagne or sparkling wine so there is always a bottle (or two) of bubbles in an ice bucket and a pitcher of orange juice for the kids. So open the patio doors, invite a crowd and enjoy what this reviving season has to offer. This menu would also be great for a small spring bridal shower.

menu

Jamón Serrano Manchego Wraps with Quince Paste

Black Pepper-Balsamic Strawberries

Asparagus, Green Onion and Feta Frittata

Overnight Croissant French Toast Bake with Coffee Rum Sauce

timeline

Night Before—Prepare French Toast Bake

Morning of—Prepare Manchego Wraps / Prepare Black Pepper-Balsamic Strawberries / Prepare Ingredients for Frittata / Prepare Coffee Rum Sauce and Refrigerate

1 Hour Before—Bake French Toast

20 Minutes Before—Bake Frittata

jamón serrano manchego wraps with quince paste

If there is one quick bite that I rely on for a party it's this astonishing blend of flavors. Manchego and quince paste is a classic combination but I like to take it a step further and wrap it with a bit of vibrant serrano ham. Manchego cheese can be found at most grocery stores, while serrano ham and quince paste are very common at specialty markets (like Whole Foods) and cheese shops. It's an impressive yet easy appetizer that finds its way onto a cheese plate almost weekly at my house.

serves 8 | prep time: 15 minutes

8 oz (226 g) Manchego cheese

¼ lb (113 g) jamón serrano, thinly sliced

Quince paste

With a sharp knife, remove the rind of the Manchego and slice the cheese into roughly sixteen ⅛-inch (3-mm) triangles. Slice the serrano in half lengthwise, then again in half, creating 4 strips of serrano out of 1 slice. Slice the quince paste into sixteen ⅛-inch (3-mm) thick rectangles.

To assemble, place one rectangle of quince paste onto a slice of Manchego and wrap with serrano. Sometimes the serrano can be too dry to wrap and if that is the case, simply place a small slice of serrano on top of the Manchego and top with quince paste. Repeat with the remaining Manchego slices and serve on a cheese board or serving plate.

This can be assembled 2 hours before serving or up to a day in advance and stored tightly wrapped with food-grade plastic wrap in the refrigerator and allowed to rest at room temperature for 1 hour before serving.

black pepper-balsamic strawberries

Like sweet jewels of the season, strawberries are spring's candy. At every gathering I like to put a bowl of ripe seasonal fruit out, and sometimes I step it up a notch by either adding complementary or contrasting flavors to make the fruit really stand out. These black pepper and balsamic strawberries are just that. Tawny and tangy balsamic vinegar with a touch of fresh ground black pepper really intensifies the flavor of these spring gems and makes for a stunning dish.

serves 8 | prep time: 10 minutes | set time: 30 minutes

2 lbs (907 g) strawberries, halved

3 tbsp (44 ml) aged balsamic vinegar

2 tbsp (24 g) granulated sugar

1½ tsp (3 g) fresh ground black pepper

In a large bowl, combine all ingredients and mix until combined. Cover and refrigerate for at least 30 minutes or up to 4 hours. Serve as is or with a touch of whipped cream.

asparagus, green onion and feta frittata

If there is one brunch recipe that I rely on to feed a group with little fuss, it's a frittata—the ultimate one-pan wonder. It's one of those recipes you can't really prepare in advance, but it's so easy and fast to put together that it's no trouble. With tender asparagus, tangy feta cheese and savory green onion, this recipe takes advantage of the fresh flavors of spring and is perfect for a party.

serves 8 | prep time: 10 minutes | cook time: 15 minutes

12 large eggs

2 tsp (10 ml) Dijon mustard

½ tsp salt

¼ tsp fresh ground black pepper

3 tbsp (45 g) unsalted butter

2 cups (203 g) thin asparagus, trimmed, cut into 1-inch (2.5-cm) pieces

2 green onions, trimmed and cut into ¼-inch (6-mm) pieces

4 oz (113 g) crumbled feta cheese

Preheat oven to 400°F (205°C).

In a large bowl, combine eggs, mustard, salt and pepper and whisk until eggs are slightly frothy, about 20 seconds.

In a 12-inch (30-cm) nonstick skillet, melt butter over medium heat. Sauté asparagus and onions until asparagus is tender, about 3 minutes. Pour egg mixture into the skillet, add feta and stir to combine all ingredients. Remove from heat, transfer to the oven and bake for 15 to 20 minutes until cooked through and a toothpick inserted into the middle comes out clean.

Separate the frittata from the skillet by running a flexible spatula around the edges of the frittata; then slide the frittata onto a serving plate or cake stand. Slice into eight wedges and serve.

suggested pairing
White wines such as Savignon Blanc, Gruner Veltliner or Verdicchio.

overnight croissant french toast bake with coffee rum sauce

Let's just start off by saying in no way is this actually French toast. Rather, it's an insanely delicious, over-the-top bread pudding hidden under the name "French toast" to technically make it a brunch recipe. Of course if I had my way, I would have this for breakfast, lunch and dinner! The beauty of this dish is that it comes together quickly, is prepared the night before and uses melted ice cream for the rum sauce base to keep it quick and simple.

serves 8 | prep time: 10 minutes | cook time: 35 minutes

french toast bake

8 croissants

4 large eggs

1½ cups (354 ml) heavy cream

½ cup (117 ml) pure maple syrup

1 tsp (5 ml) vanilla paste or extract

½ tsp ground cinnamon

¼ tsp fresh grated nutmeg

coffee rum sauce

1 cup (236 ml) coffee ice cream, melted

2 oz (59 ml) dark rum

Butter a 9 × 13-inch (23 × 33-cm) baking dish. Tear croissants into 2-inch (5-cm) pieces and set into the baking dish. In a large bowl, whisk to combine eggs, cream, maple syrup, vanilla, cinnamon and nutmeg. Pour over croissants and gently toss to make sure the croissants are coated with custard mixture. Cover and refrigerate overnight. Before baking, allow the dish to sit at room temperature for 30 minutes.

Preheat oven to 350°F (175°C). Bake uncovered for 35 to 40 minutes until golden and the custard has set but is still soft.

Combine melted coffee ice cream with dark rum and serve over the warm French Toast Bake.

notes

This does not need to be prepared overnight to be successful and can be prepared hours in advance or right before serving. Also, if serving to children, omit the rum. Vanilla ice cream could also be used or even just regular maple syrup; there are so many options here.

> lunch <

· Herbed Feta Dip

· Chive Deviled Eggs

· Shaved Asparagus Salad

· Rosemary Garlic Pork Loin
with Fingerling Potatoes

· Orange Cardamom Cookies

easter lunch

Many years ago as a child, I was forced to wear a poofy navy dress with enormous pink flowers and gargantuan shoulder pads to an Easter party. I was so upset at this monstrosity that the only relief I found was laughing at my brother's bow tie, which was cutting off his circulation so much that his face was turning red. As all children do when faced with something they don't want to do, we swore that this event would be an utter disaster and we wouldn't have any fun at all; but by the time the deviled eggs came out and the Easter egg hunt with all of our cousins started, we couldn't care less what we were wearing.

Easter is the ultimate spring celebration. Everyone is in their Sunday best laughing and sharing stories while kids are ripping through the newly budding gardens in search of goodies that an enormous pink bunny has left them the night before. Pair all of this with the fresh and bright flavors of spring and you have yourself a party.

menu

Herbed Feta Dip

Chive Deviled Eggs

Shaved Asparagus Salad

Rosemary Garlic Roasted Pork Loin with Fingerling Potatoes

Orange Cardamom Cookies

timeline

2 Days in Advance—Make Orange Cardamom Cookies

1 Day in Advance—Set Table / Make Herbed Feta Dip / Prepare Deviled Eggs / Prepare Pork Loin Roast

Morning of—Assemble Deviled Eggs / Prepare Asparagus Salad

1 Hour Before—Cook Pork Loin Roast / Chill Wine / Assemble Salad / Set out Dip

herbed feta dip

A light and tangy dip, this Herbed Feta Dip is so simple to blend together and can be made a day in advance. I like to place a bowl of this bright dip on a large platter or wooden board surrounded by sliced vegetables, toasted baguette slices and crackers for guests to snack on before lunch.

serves 12 | prep time: 10 minutes

8 oz (about 2 cups [224 g]) crumbled feta cheese

½ cup (122 g) plain yogurt

1 tbsp (9 g) fresh dill

1 tbsp (9 g) fresh parsley, chopped

1 tbsp (9 g) fresh thyme, chopped

2 tbsp (22 g) green olives, chopped

2 tbsp (22 g) pine nuts

1 tbsp (14 ml) extra virgin olive oil

Fresh ground black pepper

In a blender or food processor, blend feta and yogurt until smooth and creamy. Add dill, parsley and thyme and pulse until the herbs are just folded in.

Transfer dip into a serving bowl, cover and refrigerate until ready to serve. Just before serving, top with olives, pine nuts, a drizzle of olive oil and a pinch of black pepper. Serve with toasted baguettes, crackers and/or sliced vegetables such as bell peppers, carrots, cucumber and broccoli.

suggested pairing
Light-bodied, low-alcohol whites like Sancerre or dry German Kabinett Riesling.

chive deviled eggs

Deviled eggs, the quintessential Easter appetizer, are like palm-sized agents of glory adored by everyone from toddler to great-grandparent. I can't tell you how many recipes from the traditional to the zany I have developed for clients over the years, but by this point I've gotten it down to an exact science. I like my deviled eggs very cold so I make the eggs and filling a day in advance and assemble them the morning, keeping them in the refrigerator until I'm ready to serve.

makes 24 deviled eggs | prep time: 20 minutes | cook time: 30 minutes

12 large eggs

¼ cup (61 g) plain Greek yogurt

3 tbsp (39 g) mayonnaise

2 tbsp (30 ml) champagne or white wine vinegar

2 tsp (10 ml) Dijon mustard

2 tbsp (6 g) chopped chives

Flaked sea salt

Fill a large pot halfway with water and bring to a boil. Using a spoon, carefully drop eggs into the boiling water. Cook for 10 minutes. Remove the eggs and immediately transfer to a bowl of ice water until they are completely cool.

Lightly crack the eggs by tapping on a hard surface, then remove the shell and discard. With a knife, slice the eggs in half lengthwise. With a spoon, remove the egg yolks and place in a food processor. Place the egg whites in a sealable container and store in the refrigerator until ready to assemble.

To the yolks, add yogurt, mayonnaise, vinegar and mustard. Process until smooth and creamy, about 1 minute, then fold in 1 tablespoon (3 g) of chives. If not using a food processor, mash the egg yolks with a fork and whisk everything together until smooth. Taste and season with salt as needed. Place the mixture into a piping bag or a food storage plastic bag and store in the refrigerator until ready to assemble.

When ready to serve, place the egg whites on a serving platter. Snip the end off of the piping bag and pipe an equal amount of the egg yolk mixture into the egg. Lightly sprinkle with flaked sea salt. Top each egg with a pinch of chopped chives. Serve cold.

suggested pairing
Champagne and other dry sparkling wines.

shaved asparagus salad

The smell of fresh grass, a hint of a warm breeze and the delicate green flavors that are bountiful this time of year bring excitement into the kitchen, and to me this salad personifies them. Not only is shaved asparagus easy to create, but it's deliciously elegant and perfect for an Easter lunch. Prep all ingredients the morning before serving, shave the asparagus and pecorino and store in food-safe plastic bags in the refrigerator. Then, create the vinaigrette and store at room temperature. Assemble and plate up to an hour before guests arrive.

serves 12 | prep time: 20 minutes

2 bunches thick asparagus, ends trimmed

½ lb (226 g) prosciutto, sliced thin and torn into strips

Wedge Pecorino cheese

⅓ cup (78 ml) extra virgin olive oil

3 tbsp (44 ml) champagne or white wine vinegar

1 tsp (5 ml) Dijon mustard

Pinch salt and pepper

Old style whole-grain Dijon mustard, optional

Working with one asparagus at a time, use a vegetable peeler or mandolin to shave asparagus in to long thin strips. Equally divide the asparagus onto salad plates and top with a few strips of prosciutto. Using a vegetable peeler, shave pecorino (about 5 shavings a serving) onto asparagus.

In a large bowl, combine olive oil, vinegar, mustard, salt and pepper; whisk vigorously until combined and emulsified. Drizzle one large spoonful of vinaigrette over each serving and garnish with a few small spoonfuls of whole-grain mustard, if desired.

rosemary garlic roasted pork loin with fingerling potatoes

Here's one of our favorite simple meals that can serve a crowd easily and pleases practically anyone. Fresh rosemary combines with savory garlic and bright lemon zest to create a delicious mouthwatering rub that slowly infuses the pork loin with flavor while roasting in the oven. To make this meal even easier on myself come Easter day, I prepare the loin the night before and throw it in the oven as I'm getting ready for the party. This also makes an elegant Christmas dinner.

serves 12 | prep time: 10 minutes | cook time: 1 hour 30 minutes

2 lbs (907 g) fingerling potatoes

1 lb (453 g) carrots sliced in 2-inch (5-cm) pieces

2 tbsp (29 ml) olive oil, divided

4 cloves garlic, minced

2 tbsp (6 g) fresh rosemary, chopped

2 tbsp (29 ml) Dijon mustard

½ tbsp (8 g) kosher salt

1 tsp (1 g) grated lemon zest

½ tsp fresh ground black pepper

5-lb (2.3-kg) boneless pork loin roast

In a large roasting pan, toss potatoes and carrots with 1 tablespoon (15 ml) of olive oil and season with a pinch of salt and pepper. Place a roasting rack on top of the potatoes and carrots.

In a bowl, stir to combine garlic, rosemary, mustard, remaining olive oil, salt, lemon zest and pepper. Place the pork loin, fat side up, on the roasting rack and evenly coat it with the garlic and rosemary mixture. Cover with plastic wrap and store in the refrigerator overnight.

When ready to cook, allow the roast to sit at room temperature for 30 minutes prior to roasting. Place in a 475°F (245°C) preheated oven and roast for 30 minutes. Reduce heat to 425°F (220°C) and continue to roast for 1 hour or until the juices run clear and a cooking thermometer registers 150°F (65°C) when inserted in the center.

Transfer the pork roast to a carving board, tent with foil and allow to rest for 10 minutes before carving into thin slices. The roast should be slightly pink but cooked through. Toss the potatoes and carrots in the cooking juices at the bottom of the pan and serve with the pork.

suggested pairing

Pinot Noir, Gamay, Barbera (serve slightly chilled) or you can go to Alto Adige for a Lagrein.

note

A 5-pound (2.3-kg) pork loin roast can be hard to come by due to its size. If you can't find one, look for two 2½-pound (1.1-kg) pork loin roasts and cook accordingly.

orange cardamom cookies

Unique and delicious, these elegant cookies are flavored with beautiful cardamom, citrusy orange zest and crunchy pistachios for a sweet treat to end an Easter lunch. Being a shortbread cookie, the batter comes together quickly and is then rolled, sliced and baked for a simple but distinctive dessert.

makes 24 cookies | prep time: 15 minutes | bake time: 13 minutes

cookies

1¼ cups (156 g) all-purpose flour

¾ tsp ground cardamom

Zest from 1 large orange, grated

¼ tsp salt

½ cup (1 stick [114 g]) unsalted butter, softened

½ cup (95 g) granulated sugar

1 large egg

1 tsp (5 ml) almond extract

⅓ cup (56 g) shelled pistachios, chopped

icing

1 cup (130 g) confectioner's sugar

1 to 3 tbsp (15 to 45 ml) milk

Decorating sugar

In a medium bowl, combine flour, cardamom, orange zest and salt; set aside.

Using a stand mixer with a paddle attachment or hand mixer on a medium-high setting, cream together butter and sugar until fluffy, about 2 minutes. Add egg and almond extract and mix until combined. With the mixer on medium-low, add the flour mixture and mix until just combined, then fold in the pistachios. Place dough on a sheet of plastic wrap, shape into a 2 × 12-inch (5 × 30-cm) log and wrap with plastic wrap. Refrigerate for 30 minutes until firm.

Preheat oven to 350°F (175°C) and line a baking sheet with parchment paper. Remove the plastic wrap from the dough and slice into ⅓-inch (8-mm) thick slices. Place slices onto the baking sheet and bake for 13 to 15 minutes until slightly golden on the edges. Transfer to a cooling rack and cool.

Combine confectioner's sugar and milk, 1 tablespoon (15 ml) at a time until slightly fluid. Dip cookies, face side down until covered in icing, then top with decorating sugar. Allow to set, then store in an airtight container until ready to serve.

sunset garden party

A gentle cool breeze makes the hanging stream of lanterns dance to the music coming from my husband's guitar while the backyard is full of laughter and fresh spring blooms. These are the scenes from my favorite spring nights in our garden. As with cooking, gardening has always been a passion of mine and come springtime, I'm eager to tend to the beds again and get everything looking revived and lush. Once the herbs and vegetables break out of the earth and begin to grow, it's time to get cooking and share the bounty with our friends and neighbors.

This dinner is all about celebrating spring and finally being able to enjoy the weather again after the frigid winter. Outdoor parties are pretty casual affairs for us and this party is no exception. I like to serve the food buffet style inside the house and then have a long table set up outside adorned with flowers, tea candles and place settings. Burlap can be purchased online and makes a great rustic table runner or placemats that fit in with the garden theme.

menu

Bee's Knees Cocktail with Thyme Honey

Chilled Shrimp with Cilantro Crème Fraîche

Fava Bean and Cucumber Salad

Apricot Curry Chicken Sandwiches

Lemon Elderflower Icebox Cakes

timeline

A Week in Advance—Make Simple Syrup for Bee's Knees Cocktail

1 Day in Advance—Boil Shrimp and Make Cilantro Crème Fraîche / Prepare Ingredients for Apricot Curry Chicken Sandwiches / Make and Assemble Lemon Elderflower Icebox Cakes / Prepare Serving Table

Morning of—Prepare Fava Bean Salad

1 Hour Before—Assemble Bee's Knees Cocktail and Put on Ice / Assemble Apricot Curry Chicken Sandwiches

bee's knees cocktail with thyme honey

Back in the days of flapper dresses and bathtub gin, a cocktail called The Bee's Knees was being secretly sipped on during the grand parties of the Prohibition Era. Decades later, this famous cocktail is beginning to have a revival, and it has become one of my favorite cocktails to serve as guests arrive. I've given this simple drink a garden twist by infusing the honey syrup with beautiful thyme to complement this sweet and sour refreshing cocktail. Fair warning though; these beauties go fast—you just might want to make a double batch!

serves 8 | prep time: 10 minutes

thyme-honey syrup

¼ cup (59 ml) honey

¼ cup (59 ml) boiling hot water

4 sprigs thyme

cocktail

16 oz (2 cups [473 ml]) gin

6 oz (¾ cup [180 ml]) fresh lemon juice

4 oz (½ cup [120 ml]) thyme-honey syrup

In a heatproof container, combine honey, water and thyme and stir until the honey has dissolved. Allow to cool, then remove the thyme. This can be done a day in advance.

The key to making this cocktail spectacular is having it as cold as possible. This is traditionally done by shaking with ice in a cocktail shaker, but standing around making individual cocktails as guests enter the door can be a bit stressful. So to make this incredibly easy, combine gin, lemon juice and thyme-honey syrup in a carafe or a pitcher 30 minutes before the party and place in a bucket full of ice to get really cold. Once guests arrive, pour equally into 8 coupe glasses and garnish with a lemon peel or sprig of thyme.

chilled shrimp with cilantro crème fraîche

Sweet and succulent cold shrimp dipped in a flavorful herbed yogurt is a delicious take on the classic shrimp cocktail that was so popular decades ago. Make this delightful appetizer a day in advance and store in the refrigerator until just before serving.

serves 8 | prep time: 20 minutes | cook time: 3 minutes

shrimp

1 yellow onion, quartered

3 cloves garlic, peeled

1 tbsp (15 g) kosher salt

1 bay leaf

2 lbs (900 g) extra jumbo (16/20 count) wild shrimp

cilantro crème fraîche

1 cup (40 g) cilantro

¾ cup (177 ml) crème fraîche or sour cream

¼ cup (60 g) cream cheese

1 jalapeño, seeded

In a large pot of boiling water, add onion, garlic, salt and bay leaf; boil for 10 minutes. Add shrimp and cook until shrimp begin to slightly curl, turn pink and are cooked through, about 3 minutes. Strain from and rinse in cold water until cool to the touch. Peel the shrimp, leaving the tails intact and devein if desired. Store in an airtight container in the refrigerator until ready to serve.

To make the cilantro crème fraîche, place all ingredients in a food processor or blender and process until well combined. Store in an airtight container until ready to serve.

To serve, place shrimp on a platter with crème fraîche in a serving bowl.

suggested pairing
Grillo (a light Sicilian white), Sancerre or other cool-climate Sauvignon Blanc. Beer: extra pale, pilsner or Gose.

fava bean and cucumber salad

Along with peas, fava beans are the epitome of spring with their fresh flavor. Unfortunately, fava beans are also a serious pain to shell. For this salad, I use frozen fava beans that are already shelled, which can be purchased at most stores. If you can't find frozen fava beans, simply replace with frozen peas, lima beans or even shelled edamame.

serves 8 | prep time: 15 minutes | cook time: 4 minutes

salad

½ tbsp (8 g) kosher salt

4 cups (605 g) frozen shelled fava beans

2 cucumbers, peeled, sliced and quartered

1 cup (40 g) pea shoots, optional

2 tbsp (5 g) fresh parsley, chopped

2 oz (56 g) Manchego cheese

vinaigrette

⅓ cup (78 ml) extra virgin olive oil

¼ cup (59 ml) fresh lemon juice

1 shallot, minced

Salt and pepper

Bring a large pot of water to a boil. Add the kosher salt and fava beans and boil for 4 minutes until beans are tender. Drain and immediately place fava beans in a bowl of ice water to chill and stop the cooking process. Once cold, drain and place the fava beans in a large bowl. To the fava beans, add cucumbers, pea shoots and parsley.

In another bowl, combine olive oil, lemon juice, shallot and a pinch of salt and pepper and whisk to combine. Add the vinaigrette to the salad with Manchego and toss to combine. Serve on a large serving platter.

To make ahead, create the salad and vinaigrette separately and store in the refrigerator up to 4 hours in advance. Add the vinaigrette to the salad just before serving.

apricot curry chicken sandwiches

As far as I know, there is not a rule that says you can't serve sandwiches at a party, especially when they are sandwiches like these. Inspired by our local bahn mi shop, these easy-to-put-together sandwiches use store-bought rotisserie chicken flavored with a simple apricot-curry glaze, quick-pickled slaw, fresh cucumber and Sriracha mayo on a soft baguette for an amazing but simple meal.

serves 8 | prep time: 30 minutes

quick-pickled slaw

2 cups (681 g) carrot and cabbage slaw

½ cup (118 ml) rice or white wine vinegar

1½ tbsp (17 g) sugar

1 tsp (5 g) salt

apricot curry glaze

¼ cup (59 ml) apricot jam

3 tbsp (44 ml) water

1½ tsp (4 g) curry powder

½ tsp ground ginger

½ tsp fish sauce, optional

Pinch salt

sriracha mayonnaise

½ cup (118 ml) good-quality mayonnaise

3 tsp (15 ml) Sriracha

sandwich

8 (6-inch [15-cm]) French baguette halves

1 rotisserie chicken, meat pulled from bones and shredded

1 cucumber, sliced ⅛-inch (3-mm) thick

2 jalapeños, sliced thin

Fresh cilantro

To make the quick-pickled slaw, combine all ingredients in a bowl and allow to marinate in the refrigerator for at least 30 minutes to overnight.

To make the glaze, whisk to combine all ingredients and store in an airtight container in the refrigerator until needed.

To make the mayonnaise, whisk to combine all ingredients in a bowl and store in the refrigerator until needed.

Slice baguettes to make sandwich halves. Place a handful of chicken on the bottom half and spoon on the apricot-curry glaze. Top with cucumber slices, jalapeño, slaw and cilantro. Spread a spoonful of Sriracha mayo on the top half of the baguette and close the sandwich. Insert a toothpick in the center or wrap with parchment paper to secure. Repeat with remaining baguettes. Assemble up to an hour before party and store in the refrigerator until ready to serve.

suggested pairing

Chardonnay, especially Monterey or southern Burgundy (Macon-Villages, Pouilly-Fuisse); Beer: Asian lagers, rice beer, witbier.

lemon elderflower icebox cakes

I'd never had an icebox cake until some good friends of ours served one at their house one night. I was in complete shock that cookies and whipped cream could make an instant cake, and that family recipe of theirs has stuck with me ever since. With hints of elderflower, honey, sea salt, lemon and roasted cashews, I've created a version that is simple to make but complex in flavor. I like to use Meyer Lemon Moravian Cookies from Salem Baking Co. but any lemon cookie will do. Serve these individual cakes in clear plastic glasses for easy clean up or small parfait glasses. Either way, these delectable desserts are an impressive way to end any spring or summer meal.

serves 8 | prep time: 20 minutes

1 quart (32 oz [946 ml]) heavy whipping cream

6 tbsp (88 ml) elderflower liqueur

⅓ cup (78 ml) honey

1 tbsp (2.5 g) lemon zest

32 small lemon cookies

½ cup (55 g) roasted cashews, finely chopped

Maldon or flaked sea salt

Organic small edible flowers, optional

In a blender, food processor or stand mixer with a whisk attachment, whip cream until it just begins to thicken. Add elderflower liqueur, honey and lemon zest and whip until stiff peaks form and mixture will not fall off a spoon when held upside down. Be careful not to over whip as the cream will lose its smooth texture.

In 8 cups or small glass serving dishes, place one cookie then top with a spoonful of whipped cream. Top with another cookie and another spoonful of whipped cream; repeat 2 more times for a total of 4 cookies per cup. Cover glasses with plastic wrap and refrigerate overnight.

Place cashews in a food processor and pulse until finely chopped and it almost looks like sand.

When ready to serve, top with a spoonful of cashews, a pinch of Maldon or flaked sea salt and an edible flower. Serve.

suggested pairing:
Demi-sec bubbles; A little limoncello over cracked ice is delicious too!

coconut curry mussels

carrot ginger soup
with mint cashew pesto

roasted chicken with fennel
and leek croutons

chardonnay poached apricots

dinner with friends

I love our friends. They have to put up with my crazy schedule, constantly let me use them as taste testers and props in photography and as a consequence don't mind eating their food cold. They deserve a nice dinner from time to time that doesn't involve a serve yourself table.

I like to create a table setting that's elegant and inviting with gorgeous round spheres of white and green hydrangeas amongst twinkling tea lights. This dinner focuses on fresh spring flavors and a complex tasting but easy roasted chicken over a bright, lemony salad of leeks and fennel.

menu

Coconut Curry Mussels

Carrot Ginger Soup with Mint Cashew Pesto

Roasted Chicken with Fennel and Leek Croutons

Chardonnay Poached Apricots

timeline

2 Days in Advance—Create the Chardonnay Poached Apricots

1 Day in Advance—Create the Carrot Ginger Soup / Prepare the Roasted Chicken / Set the Table

Morning of—Create the Mint Cashew Pesto / Prepare Ingredients for Coconut Curry Mussels

1 Hour Before—Remove Roasted Chicken from the Refrigerator / Chill Wine

30 Minutes Before—Roast Chicken

coconut curry mussels

The simplicity and flavor of this dish makes up for the immediate hands-on time. I find that prepping everything in advance, like mincing the shallots and garlic, makes this dish come together fast. Briny mussels combined with delicately sweet coconut milk, lime juice and aromatic curry paste is a beautiful dish perfect for a night with friends around the table. This makes for the ideal small bite to start the night off and the perfect meal for two on date night—so keep it in your back pocket.

serves 6 | prep time: 15 minutes | cook time: 15 minutes

2 lbs (908 g) mussels

1 tbsp (15 ml) grapeseed or canola oil

2 shallots, minced

2 garlic cloves, minced

1 (6-inch [15-cm]) piece of lemongrass

3 tbsp (40 g) red curry paste

15 oz (443 ml) coconut milk

½ cup (118 ml) seafood (or chicken) stock

¼ cup (10 g) cilantro leaves

2 tbsp (30 ml) fresh lime juice

Right before your guests arrive, rinse mussels and remove the beards by gently pulling on them (if your fish monger hasn't already done so) and place mussels in a large bowl of ice-cold water in the refrigerator, about 30 minutes maximum.

Heat oil in a wok or a large sauté pan over medium heat and sauté the shallots, garlic and lemongrass for 3 minutes or until fragrant. Add curry paste, coconut milk and stock, and bring to boil over high heat. Reduce heat to medium simmer for 5 minutes. Add mussels, stir, cover and steam for about 5 to 6 minutes until the mussels completely open. Add cilantro and lime juice, then toss the mussels in the broth.

Divide between 6 serving bowls and serve immediately.

carrot ginger soup with mint cashew pesto

This velvety rich soup of sweet carrot and bright ginger with a nutty fresh pesto is an exquisite blend of flavors inspired by what is starting to pop up in my garden. This soup is simple to make, can be made a day in advance, and can be served cold or hot depending on your preference.

serves 6 | prep time: 10 minutes | cook time: 30 minutes

carrot and ginger soup

2 tbsp (10 ml) olive oil

1 yellow onion, chopped

1 clove garlic, minced

2-inch (5-cm) piece ginger, peeled and minced

2 lbs (900 g) carrots, thinly sliced

5 cups (1.2 L) chicken or vegetable stock

Salt and fresh ground black pepper

mint cashew pesto

½ cup (20 g) mint leaves, loosely packed

½ cup (56 g) roasted and salted cashews

1 garlic clove

⅓ cup (78 ml) extra virgin olive oil

1 tsp (5 ml) lemon juice

In a large 6-quart (5.6-L) pot, heat oil over medium heat. Add onion, garlic, ginger and carrots and sauté for 5 to 8 minutes until the carrots just begin to become tender. Add stock and bring to a boil over high heat. Reduce heat to a simmer, and simmer for 30 minutes until carrots are extremely tender. Working in batches, purée the soup until smooth and return to the pot. Taste and add salt and pepper as needed. Cool and store in the refrigerator until ready to serve.

To make the pesto, combine mint, cashews and garlic in a food processor and pulse until the mint and cashews are finely chopped. Stir in olive oil and lemon juice. Can be made a day in advance and stored in the refrigerator until needed but serve at room temperature. When ready to serve, spoon a dollop of pesto onto each serving of soup.

suggested pairing
Pinot Noir or Chardonnay.

roasted chicken with fennel and leek croutons

Way back in the all-night study days of college, I lived off roasted chickens, potatoes and boxed wine. It was a meal that lasted for days, but more importantly would feed all of us who were sick and tired of pizza and ramen! Fast forward many years and I still rely on a simple roasted chicken to feed my people (but I've mercifully moved past the boxed wine). For this recipe, I like to prepare everything the night before, and throw the chicken in the oven just before my guests arrive. Once the chicken, fennel and leeks are golden, I carve the chicken and toss sourdough croutons and fresh arugula with the fennel, leeks and the pan drippings for a distinctively delicious meal.

serves 6 | prep time: 25 minutes | cook time: 1 hour 25 minutes

3 leeks

2 large fennel bulbs

2 tbsp (28 ml) olive oil

2 (4-lb [1.8 kg]) whole chickens, giblets removed

4 tbsp (57 g) butter, softened

1 small (about 1 lb [454 g]) sourdough loaf, sliced into 1-inch (2.5-cm) cubes

3 tsp (15 g) kosher salt

2 tsp (10 g) fresh ground black pepper

3 cups arugula

1 tbsp (14 ml) fresh lemon juice

suggested pairing

Albariño, Pinot Gris from Oregon's Willamette Valley.

Remove the green parts and roots from the leeks. Slice the white part of the leeks in half lengthwise and rinse under running water. This will help remove any sand in the leeks. Slice the leeks in 2-inch (5-cm) sections and place in a large roasting pan. Remove any stalks and fronds from the fennel and slice the fennel bulbs into 6 wedges each; reserve ¼ cup (85 g) of the fronds. Place fennel with the leeks in the roasting pan and toss with 1 tablespoon (15 ml) olive oil. If you have a roasting rack, place it on top of the leeks and fennel.

Gently separate the skin over the chicken breasts from the meat with your hands and place a tablespoon (15 g) of butter on each chicken breast. With cooking twine, tie the legs of the chickens together (optional) and place chickens, breast side up, on the roasting rack; refrigerate, uncovered, overnight. Refrigerating the chickens uncovered makes for a beautifully crisp skin and can be done the morning of, if needed.

To make the croutons, toast the sourdough cubes in a preheated 350°F (175°C) oven for 15 minutes until toasted. Store at room temperature until needed.

Remove the roasting pan from the refrigerator and allow to come to room temperature 40 minutes prior to cooking; season each chicken with 1½ teaspoons (8 g) salt and 1 teaspoon (5 g) pepper. Preheat oven to 425°F (220°C) and roast the chickens, fennel and leeks for 1 hour and 25 minutes or until a thermometer inserted into the thigh reaches 165°F (73°C). Place chickens on a carving board and allow to rest for 10 minutes before carving.

Add the croutons to the fennel and leeks and add arugula, lemon juice and reserved fennel fronds; toss to combine and season with salt and pepper if necessary.

Carve the chickens and plate each serving with the croutons or place the croutons on a large platter with the carved chicken arranged on top.

chardonnay poached apricots

It's rare that cooking a fruit makes it reach its full potential, but to me cooked apricots are tastier than fresh ones. I could be a little biased because I grew up on my nanny's famous fried apricot pies, but I'm sticking to my guns on this one. These sweet wine and vanilla poached apricots are a heavenly explosion of fruit and a delightful way to end this spring meal. Apricots are just coming into season in April and if you can't get your hands on any, spring cling peaches are a good substitute.

serves 6 | prep time: 15 minutes | cook time: 5 minutes

1 vanilla bean pod, sliced in half lengthwise

2 cups (472 ml) chardonnay

½ cup (95 g) sugar

9 ripe yet firm apricots, halved and pitted

Scrape seeds from the vanilla bean pod and place the seeds along with the pod in a 2-quart (1.9-L) sauté pan with chardonnay and sugar. Bring to a boil over high heat and boil for 1 minute until the sugar is dissolved.

Add apricots and reduce heat to a slow simmer. Simmer for 4 to 5 minutes, gently stirring halfway through, until apricots are tender but still hold their shape.

Transfer apricots and syrup to a bowl to cool then cover and refrigerate until ready to serve. Serve 3 apricot halves and a spoonful of syrup per person and serve as is or with a spoonful of cream and almond slivers. Can be made up to 2 days in advance.

summer

Ah, the lazy days of summer when the sweltering heat can make an afternoon pool party run late into the cooling hours of the night. Grills get lit, boiling pots get heated and coolers get filled (and then emptied) as we mingle in the backyard amongst the kids' games of tag and epic water balloon battles. These are the days I live for and cherish having. Summer is the best time to enjoy the most casual of gatherings outside and escape the heat indoors with more quiet events around the dinner table.

backyard seafood boil

I live nowhere near the ocean, but the other day I stepped on a mussel shell in my backyard and was instantly taken back to our most recent seafood boil. Great friends, music, bright red crabs, shrimp, clams, plenty of libations to go around and lots of laughter under a vibrant setting summer sun. Out of all of the parties and celebrations we've ever thrown, seafood boils are my absolute favorite. There's a unique fun to a seafood boil that makes everyone inherently have a good time. It's all about lots of food, complete and utter casualness, eating with your hands, enjoying the outdoors and the joyous fact that I don't have to do the dishes. The most important part is inviting good people who don't mind getting their hands dirty and having plenty of paper napkins on hand.

You will need a 10 to 15 gallon (38 to 57 L) pot with a basket and an outdoor propane stove. You can easily find one online and with a little looking, can find a great package deal for under $100. I found our setup at a flea market for $50 and it was worth every cent. You will also need a long table, disposable plastic tablecloths or butcher paper, napkins and crab mallets (also available on Amazon). I cover my table with several layers of butcher paper, set out a few mason jars full of flowers and make sure there are a few bowls set out for guests to discard shells and we're ready to pour our hot fresh seafood on to the table and dig in. Once we're finished, everything is wrapped up and thrown away—the perfect easy clean up after an amazing meal.

menu

IPA Quick-Pickle Green Beans

Fennel Bread

Seafood Boil

Sorbet and Prosecco

timeline

1 Week in Advance—Pickle Green Beans

1 Day in Advance—Plate Sorbet and Freeze / Check Equipment

Morning of—Purchase Seafood, Store Crabs in an Open Cooler with Wet Newspaper and Store Remaining Seafood in Refrigerator / Prepare Bread / Prepare Vegetables and Sausages for Seafood Boil

30 Minutes Before—Begin Boiling Water / Ice Down Drinks

IPA quick-pickle green beans

I have a group of beer-enthusiast friends and a beer snob of a husband. Needless to say, I have access to all sorts of craft beer and one day, an India Pale Ale (IPA) found its way into some green beans I was pickling. The result was truly enticing. Bright, tangy and flavorful, these pickled green beans make a delicious accompaniment to a seafood boil. For best results, make them a few days in advance and serve them right in the mason jar with a fork for easy retrieval.

makes 4 pint-sized (500 ml) jars | prep time: 30 minutes

8 sprigs dill

8 cloves garlic, peeled

4 bay leaves

4 tsp (11 g) coriander seeds

4 tsp (11 g) mustard seeds

2 tsp (6 g) peppercorns

2 lbs (908 g) green beans, trimmed of their ends

2 cups (16 oz [472 ml]) India Pale Ale

2 cups (472 ml) white wine vinegar

1 cup (236 ml) water

¼ cup (48 g) sugar

2 tbsp (30 g) kosher salt

Special Equipment: 4 pint-sized (500 ml) mason jars

In each jar, place 2 sprigs dill, 2 garlic cloves, 1 bay leaf, 1 teaspoon (3 g) coriander seeds, 1 teaspoon (3 g) mustard seeds, ½ teaspoon peppercorns and as many green beans as you can standing up.

In a saucepan, combine IPA, vinegar, water, sugar and salt and bring to a rapid boil. Remove from heat and carefully pour the mixture into the pint jars leaving ½-inch (13-mm) headspace. Seal the jars and allow to cool. Once room temperature, store in the refrigerator for up to 1 week.

fennel bread

When it comes to seafood boils, a must-follow rule is to have a crusty loaf of hot bread on the table, but I like to step it up and serve a quick-made fennel bread. A golden toasted crust surrounds warm soft bread with fennel-laced salted butter for an easy but elevated dinner bread that takes mere minutes to make. This bread leaves the table fast so I make sure to make two loaves when I have a large crowd.

makes 2 loaves | prep time: 10 minutes | cook time: 15 minutes

2 batards or other crusty French bread

½ cup (1 stick [114 g]) unsalted butter, softened

3 tbsp (64 g) fennel bulb, grated

1 tbsp (2.5 g) fennel fronds

1 tsp (10 g) fennel seed

1 tsp (5 g) sea salt

Preheat oven 325°F (165°C).

Without cutting all the way through the loaf (leaving the base intact), slice the bread into 1-inch (2.5-cm) thick slices.

In a bowl, combine butter, fennel, fennel seed and salt. Spread butter mixture in between slices. Place each loaf of bread on a sheet of foil and wrap foil around the sides, leaving the top of the loaf exposed.

Place bread in the oven and bake for 15 to 20 minutes until butter is melted throughout and the top of the bread is toasty. Serve immediately.

seafood boil

There is something spectacular about a seafood boil. We like to have them all throughout the summer but most of all at the beginning and end of the season when the night breeze is just a little cooler.

serves 10 to 12 | prep time: 30 minutes | cook time: 18 minutes

⅓ cup (45 g) coriander seeds

⅓ cup (45 g) mustard seeds

3 tbsp (25 g) black peppercorns

3 tbsp (20 g) celery seed

2 tbsp (16 g) allspice, whole

2 tbsp (16 g) red pepper flakes

2 tbsp (15 g) smoked paprika

6 bay leaves

4 yellow onions, sliced in half

3 lemons, sliced in half

2 heads garlic, sliced in half crosswise

½ cup (120 g) kosher salt

2 lbs (908 g) small red new potatoes

5 ears corn, husks removed and sliced in half

1 lb (454 g) smoked pork sausages, sliced into 2-inch (5-cm) sections

10 gulf coast blue crab

2 lbs (908 g) wild-caught shrimp

1 lb (405 g) mussels, rinsed of any sand

1 lb (405 g) littleneck clams, rinsed of any sand and debearded if necessary

Special Equipment: cheesecloth, 10- to 15-gallon (38- to 57-liter) pot, outdoor propane stove

In a large bowl, combine coriander seeds, mustard seeds, peppercorns, celery seeds, allspice and red pepper flakes. Place in a large square of cheesecloth, gather the corners and tie off with cooking twine. Set aside until needed.

Fill a 10- to 15-gallon (38- to 57-liter) pot fitted with a basket half full of water and begin to bring to a boil over high heat 30 minutes prior to cooking. It will take a long time for this amount of water to reach boiling point so plan accordingly. Once boiling, add spice bag, paprika, bay leaves, onions, lemons, garlic and salt and boil for 15 minutes.

Add potatoes and corn and boil for 5 minutes. Next, add sausages, crab, shrimp, mussels and clams and boil for 10 to 12 minutes or until the corn and potatoes are tender and mussels and clams have opened (discard any unopened ones). Lift out the basket, drain and pour everything onto a newspaper or butcher paper lined table.

suggested pairing

Muscadet. Also, any dry sparkling will do; Cava from Spain seems to be best with shellfish. Or, break out the beer—Pilsner, Saison, California Common, American pale ale—the choices are numerous.

sorbet and prosecco

For an incredibly easy and fast dessert in the summer, I rely on this simple recipe. When combined, sorbet and prosecco is an instant lively dessert; think of it as an adult float if you will. It's fitting on a warm summer night after a seafood—boil—and when served in disposable glasses, is as easy to clean up as the dinner.

serves 10 | prep time: 10 minutes

1 pint (473 ml) blackberry sorbet

1 pint (473 ml) peach sorbet

1 bottle (750 ml) prosecco

With an ice cream scoop, dish out a few small melon-ball-sized scoops of sorbet per serving glass. Store in the freezer until needed. Just before serving, pour ¼ cup (60 ml) prosecco over the sorbet and serve.

fiesta taco bar

Living in Texas, summer fiestas are easy to come by. Just walk down the street and the succulent smells of carnitas simmering away or barbacoa slow roasting are likely to beckon. Being so close to Mexico, Texas is infused with the savory spices and flavors of our neighbor country. On a weekend, finding a pot of meat braising in chilies is just as typical as a brisket smoking tenderly on a pit in a backyard.

You can find practically any dish at a fiesta, but tacos have an intense cult following these days and are incredibly easy to make for a crowd; this is usually what we serve. A few years back, my quite possibly insane husband decided to start a long-distance running career by running the Western States 100-mile Endurance Run, and when he finished (alive) and we made it back home, we invited everyone we knew for an epic celebratory taco party. It's a great way to serve a lot of people, and who doesn't love tacos? A few days before, I braised carnitas, simmered chicken in chilies and garlic and prepared all of the toppings. Then, when it came time to open our doors and pour ice-cold margaritas, all I had to do was enjoy the party.

Set up a large serving table with chips, guacamole, taco fillings, fresh warm tortillas and plenty of taco topping options (in Texas we call these "fixins") like pickled onion, chopped white onion, cilantro, fresh sliced jalapeños and a variety of salsas ranging from ripping hot to mild and tangy. This is certainly a casual affair, so make it as much of a self-serve station as possible and enjoy.

menu

Smoked Sea Salt Mescal Margaritas

Oven Elotes

Quick-Pickled Onions

Tomatillo and Avocado Salsa

Beer-Braised Carnitas

Mango Granita with Honeyed Buttermilk

timeline

3 Days in Advance—Pickle Onions / Create Simple Syrup for Margaritas / Create Mango Granita

2 Days in Advance—Create Avocado Tomatillo Salsa

1 Day in Advance—Braise Carnitas / Prepare Ingredients for Oven Elotes

Morning of—Plate Mango Granita in Serving Glasses and Keep Frozen / Rim Cocktail Glasses with Salt

30 Minutes Prior—Reheat Beer-Braised Carnitas / Broil Oven Elotes and Keep Warm

smoked sea salt mescal margaritas

What's a fiesta without a pitcher of margaritas? When it comes to this delicious summer concoction, skipping the premade mix and opting for tried and true real ingredients is the only way to go. For our favorite margarita that makes our guests beg for more, we swapped out traditional tequila for a high-quality smoky mescal, removed the orange liqueur so as not to overpower the beautiful smokiness and added smoked sea salt for an extraordinary cocktail.

makes 8 (4-ounce [120-ml]) servings | prep time: 10 minutes

1½ cups (355 ml) water

1 cup (192 g) sugar

1½ cups (355 ml) mescal

1 cup (236 ml) fresh lime juice, plus more for rimming glasses

Smoked sea salt

Bring water and sugar to a simmer in a pot over medium heat; stir often. Once the sugar has dissolved, remove the simple syrup from heat and cool.

Combine simple syrup, mescal and lime juice in a pitcher and refrigerate until ready to serve.

Fill a small saucer with lime juice and another saucer with smoked sea salt. Dip a lowball glass rim into the lime juice then immediately into the sea salt, pressing firmly so the salt adheres to the rim. Repeat with remaining glasses. Fill glasses carefully with ice and pour margarita over ice. Serve.

oven elotes

When I'm downtown at the farmers' market I always make sure to grab an Elote en Vaso, or corn in a cup. It is the most simple yet amazing blend of summer flavors, and whenever we have a dinner with south-of-the-border flavors, I make sure to serve this simplified recipe that doesn't involve me lighting a grill. Both the corn and cream can be prepared in advance and combined before serving. Hot, fresh sweet corn blanketed in zesty cream, lime, cheese and cilantro makes an enticing side for tacos!

serves 8 | prep time: 15 minutes | cook time: 10 minutes

½ cup (60 g) crumbled cotija or Parmesan cheese

⅓ cup (79 ml) quality mayonnaise

⅓ cup (79 ml) Mexican crema or sour cream

Zest of 1 lime, grated

2 tbsp (28 ml) lime juice

1 tbsp (8 g) chili powder

¼ cup (10 g) cilantro, chopped

10 corn cobs, husk removed

In a large bowl, mix to combine cheese, mayonnaise, crema, lime zest, lime juice, chili powder and cilantro.

With a knife, slice corn kernels off of corn cobs and place kernels on a large rimmed baking sheet. Place under the broiler and cook until corn is warmed through, begins to char and is slightly blackened, about 5 to 8 minutes. Add hot corn to the crema and mayonnaise mixture and fold until combined. Taste and add salt as needed.

Serve in a serving bowl or individual cups.

quick pickled onion

Crisp and bright, these easily made onions make for an incredible garnish and bring amazing contrasting flavor to carnitas. You can always find a jar of these beauties in my fridge in the summer months and they are great on salads, gazpacho, sandwiches—so much more than just tacos. Make them up to one week in advance.

makes 1 pint (224 g) | prep time: 10 minutes

1 red onion, halved and sliced into ⅛-inch (3-mm) thick slices

½ cup (118 ml) rice or white wine vinegar

1½ tbsp (18 g) granulated sugar

1 tsp (5 g) kosher salt

Pack onions into a pint-sized (500-ml) glass jar.

In a bowl, combine vinegar, sugar and salt and whisk until sugar is dissolved. Pour over onions, seal the jar and refrigerate for at least 2 hours or overnight, preferred. Serve with carnitas.

tomatillo and avocado salsa

A fresh salsa is a beautiful thing and I had a hard time choosing which one of my favorites would make this book. From fiery and smoky to bright and fresh, a handmade salsa can drastically transform a meal. One of my favorites comes from my time perusing the taco carts in Waco, Texas where tomatillo sauce is king. This salsa is so simple to make, but with flavors of refreshing tomatillo, creamy avocado, zesty lime and green cilantro it is complex in nature.

makes 2 cups (518 g) | prep time: 10 minutes

8 oz (226 g) tomatillos (about 4 to 5), husks removed and quartered

1 clove garlic

⅓ cup (13 g) cilantro, chopped

3 tbsp (44 g) fresh lime juice

1 serrano pepper, with seeds and ribs removed

⅛ tsp kosher salt

1 large Hass avocado, pitted

In a blender, purée tomatillos, garlic, cilantro, lime juice, serrano and salt until smooth. Add avocado and purée until blended and smooth.

Make up to 2 days in advance and store in a sealed container in the refrigerator until needed.

beer-braised carnitas

If there is one recipe that my family and friends have demanded I put in this book, this is it. I've kept it to myself for years as I've never taken time to write down the recipe. Traditionally, carnitas is one of those labor of love recipes that involves dicing a pork shoulder and then simmering it for hours in added lard, orange juice, spices and onions while tending to it every few minutes, shredding it and frying it to a crisp. Although I love a traditional recipe, I've been making this simplified version for the past 10 years and adore it just as much. This complexly flavored pork shoulder, tenderized by braising in beer and its own juices, is just as easy to make as it is to love. Make it a day in advance for easy serving.

serves 8 | prep time: 20 minutes | cook time: 4 hours

5-lb (2.2-kg) bone-in pork shoulder

1 tbsp (15 g) kosher salt

1 tsp (5 g) fresh ground black pepper

1 tbsp (14 ml) grapeseed or canola oil

12 oz (340 ml) Mexican lager or pilsner

5 cloves garlic, peeled

1 yellow onion, peeled and quartered

1 orange, sliced

1 tsp (1 g) dried oregano

1 tsp (2.5 g) cumin

2 bay leaves

Preheat oven to 325°F (165°C).

Season pork shoulder with salt and pepper. In a large 6-quart (5.6-L) heavy bottomed pot, heat oil over high heat. Sear pork on all sides until browned, about 4 minutes a side.

Once browned, place pork fat side up and add beer, garlic, onion, orange, oregano, cumin and bay leaves. Bring to a boil, cover with a lid and transfer to the oven. Braise in the oven for 4 hours or until meat is falling off the bone.

Remove from the oven and allow to cool. Shred the meat, discard the bone, orange slices and bay leaves, and return the meat to the cooking juices. Refrigerate overnight.

Ten minutes before serving, transfer meat onto a large rimmed baking sheet and place under the broiler until pork is warmed through and crispy.

Serve with warmed corn or flour tortillas with pickled onion and salsa.

suggested pairing

Margaritas, Malbec or Zinfandel, Mexican or Vienna Lager.

mango granita with honeyed buttermilk

After a meal of bold and smoldering flavors, a refreshingly chilly, fruity dessert can be a thing of beauty. This incredibly simple dessert of flaked icy mango with sweet and vivid honeyed buttermilk is a delicious end to a summer meal.

serves 8 | prep time: 5 minutes | freeze time: 4 hours

mango granita

5 cups (899 g) cubed ripe mango (about 5 mangos)

1½ cups (355 ml) water

3 tbsp (3 6g) sugar

honeyed buttermilk

¾ cup (177 ml) buttermilk

¼ cup (59 ml) honey

Mint, for garnish

In a blender or food processor, combine mango, water and sugar; purée until smooth. Pour into a 9 × 13-inch (23 × 33-cm) baking dish and freeze for 1 hour. With the tines of a fork, scrape the purée to break it up and form the icy flaked mango. Continue this process, scraping every hour, until completely frozen and flaky, about 4 hours. Once the mixture resembles shaved ice, store it in an airtight container in the freezer for up to 1 week.

To create the honeyed buttermilk, stir both buttermilk and honey until combined.

To serve, equally divide the granita into 8 glasses or serving bowls and spoon honeyed buttermilk over. Garnish with a mint leaf if desired.

menu

Chorizo Gougéres

Gazpacho with Lobster Relish

Garlic and Rosemary Roasted Salmon

Sautéed Green Beans with Miso-Mustard Vinaigrette

Vanilla Bean and Bourbon Peaches

summer soirée

You've certainly heard the old expression about the dog days of summer, but when it gets hot here in Texas, even the dog doesn't want to move unless absolutely necessary. With our high heat and humidity to match, the middle six weeks of the hot season are downright oppressive. The last thing we're in the mood for is heavy food, so the following is a collection of lighter fare that won't weigh you down while you slog through the doldrums.

I've kept the flavors varied, with a couple of nods toward traditional Spanish tapas. There's also a refreshing zip to the green beans, and I had to include a salmon dish after spending part of last summer in Cordova, Alaska, home of Copper River salmon. Finally, peaches find their way into the mix—when I met my husband, he was living in Stonewall, Texas; the renowned peaches from Gillespie County have no equal and I've never gotten over them.

menu

Chorizo Gougéres

Gazpacho with Lobster Relish

10-Minute Garlic and Rosemary Roasted Salmon

Sautéed Green Beans with Miso-Mustard Vinaigrette

Vanilla Bean and Bourbon Peaches

timeline

1 Week in Advance—Make and Freeze Chorizo Gougéres

1 Day in Advance—Prepare Gazpacho and Vanilla Bean and Bourbon Peaches / Blanch Green Beans

Morning of—Prepare Rosemary Roasted Salmon to be Cooked

30 Minutes Prior—Chill Wine

chorizo gougéres

Like crisp clouds of pastry, gougéres are an elegant hors d'oeuvre to serve. My favorite sausage to eat in the summer is a Spanish chorizo with its smoked paprika and lemony flavor, so it was no surprise that it made for an amazing take on this traditionally French appetizer. Although gougéres take a bit of hand work to prepare, the fact that you can make and freeze them in advance with a quick reheat makes this appetizer perfect for a dinner party.

makes 25 | prep time: 20 minutes | cook time: 25 minutes

½ cup (118 ml) whole milk

½ cup (118 ml) water

½ cup (1 stick [114 g]) unsalted butter

½ tsp salt

1 cup (125 g) flour

4 eggs at room temperature

1 cup (120 g) gruyere cheese, shredded

¾ cup (85g) Spanish chorizo, diced small

Position oven racks to separate the oven in thirds. Preheat oven to 425°F (220°C) and prepare 2 baking sheets by lining them with parchment paper.

In a medium non-stick saucepan over medium-high heat, bring milk, water, butter and salt to a boil. Once boiling, add flour and beat vigorously with a wooden spoon until the batter comes together, is very smooth and pulls away from the sides of the pan, about 3 to 4 minutes.

Transfer the dough to a stand mixer with a paddle attachment or in a bowl using an electric hand mixer. Allow the dough to rest and cool slightly for 2 minutes. On medium speed, add the eggs one at a time. Add cheese and chorizo and mix until just combined.

Using a tablespoon or small ice cream scoop, drop spoonfuls of the batter onto the prepared baking sheets about 2 inches (5 cm) apart. Place the baking sheets in the oven, reduce heat to 375°F (190°C) and bake for 15 minutes. Rotate the sheets and bake for an additional 10 to 15 minutes until golden.

Allow to cool then store in the freezer in a sealed plastic bag until ready to serve. As guests are arriving, reheat gougéres in a preheated 425°F (220°C) oven for 5 minutes until warmed.

suggested pairing

Sherry, a nutty Palo Cortado or Manzanilla, served chilled.

gazpacho with lobster relish

Every summer our garden bursts with beautiful tomatoes and they get put to good use in this soup. Fresh with vibrant flavors of summer, this gazpacho takes mere minutes to prepare and is a stunningly enjoyable starter to this meal.

serves 6 | prep time: 10 minutes

gazpacho

3 lbs (1.4 kg) ripe tomatoes, chopped

1 red bell pepper, seeded and chopped

1 cucumber, peeled and chopped

1 shallot, peeled and chopped

½ cup (20 g) parsley leaves

½ cup (118 ml) extra virgin olive oil

⅓ cup (78 ml) quality red wine vinegar

½ tsp kosher salt

¼ tsp fresh ground black pepper

lobster relish

6 oz (170 g) cooked and chilled lobster meat*

¼ cup (40 g) cucumber, peeled and diced

2 tbsp (28 ml) extra virgin olive oil

½ tbsp (1 g) fresh parsley, finely chopped

½ tbsp (1 g) fresh chives, finely chopped

1 tsp (5 ml) fresh lemon juice

In a blender, combine the tomatoes, red bell pepper, cucumber, shallot, parsley, olive oil, vinegar, salt and pepper and purée until slightly smooth but still has some texture. Taste and add additional salt and pepper if necessary. Place in the refrigerator for at least an hour before serving or overnight (preferred).

Chop lobster into ½-inch (13-mm) cubes and place in a bowl with cucumber, olive oil, parsley, chives, lemon juice and a pinch of salt and pepper; toss to combine.

When ready to serve, divide gazpacho into 6 bowls and top with lobster relish. Serve chilled.

note

I'm fortunate to have a market nearby that sells fresh cooked lobster; this is pretty common in specialty markets. You can always boil a lobster ahead of time or substitute cooked crab or shrimp if lobster is not available.

suggested pairing

A tart Spanish rosé will stand up to the acidity in the tomatoes. Chill it to the same temperature as your gazpacho.

10-minute garlic and rosemary roasted salmon

With its vivid pink and orange hue, tender meat and delicately balanced flavor, salmon is the star of summer. I adore its flavor and find that it's incredibly simple to cook, especially when throwing a dinner party. Simple in technique but full of flavor, garlic and rosemary roasted salmon is an exquisitely seasoned meal that takes only minutes to prepare.

serves 6 | prep time: 8 minutes | cook time: 10 minutes

6 (8-ounce [224-g]) wild-caught sockeye salmon fillets

1 tbsp (14 ml) olive oil

2 garlic cloves, minced

1½ tbsp (4 g) fresh rosemary, chopped

1 tsp (5 g) sea salt

½ tsp fresh ground black pepper

Allow salmon to rest at room temperature 20 minutes prior to roasting. Preheat oven to 425°F (220°C).

Place salmon on a parchment-lined baking sheet. Evenly top each fillet with oil, garlic, rosemary, salt and pepper. Bake for 10 to 12 minutes or until the salmon flakes easily with a fork. Serve.

note

Salmon can be prepared, covered with plastic wrap and stored in the refrigerator the morning prior to roasting.

suggested pairing

Salmon and Pinot Noir are the best of friends. Think, "what grows together goes together" and aim straight for Oregon and the Pacific Northwest. For beer, Belgian styles: Saison, Golden, Tripel.

sautéed green beans with miso-mustard vinaigrette

Green and grassy, green beans are the perfect pairing with salmon. Add a surprise vinaigrette made of a mildly sweet white shiro miso, Dijon mustard and bright sherry vinegar and you have an amazing side dish. Blanch the green beans a day in advance to help with dinner prep then simply give them a quick sauté and a toss in the vinaigrette to serve.

serves 6 | prep time: 15 minutes | cook time: 5 minutes

1½ lbs (680 g) green beans, trimmed

1 tbsp (14 ml) non-flavored oil such as grapeseed or canola

2 tsp (10 ml) white shiro miso

2 tsp (10 ml) Dijon mustard

1 tsp (5 ml) sherry vinegar

Cook green beans in a large pot of boiling salted water until tender yet crisp, about 3 to 4 minutes. Drain and place in a bowl of ice water. Remove the beans and store in an airtight container in the refrigerator until ready to serve.

Just before serving, mix oil, miso, Dijon mustard and vinegar in a bowl and set aside until needed.

Place green beans and vinaigrette in a large sauté pan and cook on medium-high until heated through, about 5 minutes. Taste and add salt and pepper as needed. Serve.

vanilla bean and bourbon peaches

Summer peaches are my weakness and bourbon is one of my many passions. Put them together and I'll be your friend for life. Sweet fresh peaches, bursting with the flavor of vanilla bean and a touch of bourbon, make a simple and elegant dessert. Serve these delicious peaches alone or with a spoonful of fresh honey-kissed whipped cream and crumbled amoretti cookies to really take this to the next level.

serves 6 | prep time: 10 minutes | marinate time: 1 hour

bourbon peaches

2 lbs (908 g) ripe peaches, pit removed and sliced into ½-inch (13-mm) slices

2½ tbsp (37 ml) quality bourbon

2 tbsp (28 g) brown sugar

1 tsp (5 ml) fresh lemon juice

1 vanilla bean pod

honeyed whipped cream

1 cup (236 ml) heavy whipping cream

2 tbsp (30 ml) honey

Crumbled amoretti cookies for serving, optional

In a large bowl, combine peaches, bourbon, sugar and lemon juice. With a sharp knife, slice the vanilla bean pod in half lengthwise and use the edge of the knife blade to scrape vanilla beans out of the pod. Place both vanilla pod and beans into the bowl. With a spatula or spoon, fold the peaches until the mixture is thoroughly combined. Cover and refrigerate for at least 1 hour. Can be made up to 3 hours in advance of serving.

If serving with whipped cream, place cream in a food processor or blender on medium speed and blend until the cream just begins to thicken. Add honey and continue blending until the whipped cream is thick and doesn't fall off a spoon when turned upside down. Can be made one day in advance.

Before serving, gently stir peaches to incorporate the syrup that has developed at the bottom of the bowl. Place peaches in a small serving dish with a dollop of whipped cream and a large pinch of amoretti crumbs.

suggested pairing

A craft bourbon or American whisky.

indian summer cookout

The kids are back in school, and the days are still boiling hot, but the sun has slipped a little to the south, and those last couple of hours before dark have begun to show a little mercy—this is one of our favorite times of year to light the grill. Here in Texas, the September cookout is as big a tradition as Friday night lights. Our summer tomatoes are still going strong, and the chile harvest is in full swing; what better companions could a grilled steak have?

The key to entertaining outside with a grill is to have everything prepped in advance and ready in the order it's going to hit the grill. This is a casual affair so paper napkins are a must and big tin tanks filled with ice and beverages should be bountiful. Think lanterns, tiki torches and a few buckets of summer flowers, and maybe a game of horseshoes. These are the times we usually break out the guitars, but if no one is that inclined, pull that speaker outside and get a playlist going.

menu

Blistered Shishito Peppers with Sea Salt and Fish Sauce

Heirloom Tomatoes and Burrata

Grilled Flat Iron with Pineapple-Avocado Salsa

Chipotle Roasted Potatoes

No-Churn Caramelized White Chocolate Ice Cream

timeline

1 Week in Advance—Create Caramelized White Chocolate Ice Cream

Morning of—Make Chipotle Roasted Potatoes / Prepare Pineapple Avocado Salsa / Plate Ice Cream and Freeze

1 Hour Before—Create Heirloom Tomato Salad / Prepare Shishitos and Steaks for Grilling

blistered shishito peppers with sea salt and fish sauce

We grow and eat a lot of peppers, and shishitos have to be my favorite. They have a beautiful vegetal taste with just a small touch of heat. When grilled and blistered, the flavor triples, and they are beautiful to serve just by themselves with a touch of sea salt and fish sauce, which complements the brightness of the peppers. Get these on the grill first and let everyone chow down before getting the steaks on.

serves 8 | prep time: 5 minutes | cook time: 4 mintues

2 lbs (908 g) shishito peppers

2 tbsp (28 ml) grapeseed or canola oil

Bamboo skewers

1 tbsp (14 ml) fish sauce

1 tsp (5 g) flaked sea salt

Toss peppers in oil. Hold two bamboo skewers parallel to each other and skewer as many peppers onto it as fit, about 8. Repeat until all peppers are used.

Preheat a gas or charcoal grill to high heat. Place skewers on the grill and cook until blistered on both sides, about 2 minutes a side. Season with fish sauce and salt; serve.

suggested pairing

Chilled Albariño or Torrontes for wine or Gose for beer.

heirloom tomatoes and burrata

This dish is a classic combination of creamy fresh mozzarella paired with acidic, fruity tomatoes and sweet, syrupy aged balsamic. I use the tomatoes straight out of our garden and plate in a large rimmed platter with a toasted baguette and watch everyone dive in. I adore its simplicity and the freshness just screams summer.

serves 8 | prep time: 10 minutes

6 heirloom tomatoes, cubed

1 (8-oz [226-g]) burrata ball, room temperature

2 tbsp (5 g) fresh basil, thinly sliced

2 tbsp (28 ml) extra virgin olive oil

2 tbsp (28 ml) aged balsamic vinegar

Flaked sea salt

Fresh ground black pepper

In a large, rimmed serving platter, arrange tomatoes. Place burrata on top then sprinkle basil over the entire dish. Just before serving, drizzle with olive oil and vinegar and season with a pinch of salt and pepper.

suggested pairing

White wines such as Pinot Grigio, Pinot Bianco or Frascati.

grilled flat iron with pineapple-avocado salsa

Tender, savory, flame-kissed steak with a smoky dry rub and a refreshing pineapple salsa is the ultimate summer satisfier! Serve family style on a large platter or cutting board with the salsa spooned over top for a gorgeous presentation.

serves 8 | prep time: 20 minutes | cook time: 8 minutes

2 tbsp (15 g) cumin

2 tbsp (15 g) smoked paprika

2 tsp (10 g) kosher salt

1 tsp (5 g) fresh ground black pepper

2 (1½-lb [675-g]) flat iron steaks

pineapple-avocado salsa

1 cup (180 g) pineapple, diced

1 cup (180 g) avocado, diced

¼ cup (38 g) red onion, diced

2 tbsp (5 g) cilantro, chopped

2 tbsp (10 g) lime juice

1 tsp (5 ml) honey

Combine cumin, paprika, salt and pepper. Equally divide and season flank steaks. Place on a baking sheet, cover and refrigerate for at least 1 hour.

In a bowl, combine pineapple, avocado, cilantro, lime juice and honey. Can be made hours in advance and refrigerated.

Preheat a gas or charcoal grill to medium-high heat. Grill steaks 4 minutes a side for medium-rare then transfer to a carving board and allow to rest for 5 minutes. Slice on the bias (cross grain) in ½-inch (13-mm)-wide strips and serve on a platter garnished with salsa.

suggested pairing

Smoky Syrah beats Cabernet for pairing with grilled meat (the Aussies call it Shiraz). Northern Rhone, Barossa Valley, California's Central Coast—it's all good.

chipotle roasted potatoes

A favorite on SteeleHouseKitchen.com, these chipotle roasted potatoes are a fiery, zesty blend of flavors perfect for a backyard late summer party. This recipe came together one night years ago when heading to a neighbor's house for a barbecue, and I needed something unique. It was a hit, and we've been making them ever since!

serves 8 | prep time: 10 minutes | cook time: 35 minutes

2 lbs (908 g) small new potatoes, sliced in half

1 tbsp (15 ml) + 2 tsp (10 ml) extra virgin olive oil

½ tsp kosher salt

1 chipotle pepper, minced, from a can of chipotle peppers in adobo sauce

2 tsp (10 ml) adobo sauce

1 garlic clove, minced

1 tbsp (9 g) lime zest, grated

1 tbsp (15 ml) fresh lime juice

2 tbsp (5 g) fresh chopped cilantro

Preheat oven to 400°F (205°C).

Place the potatoes on a baking sheet. Drizzle 1 tablespoon (15 ml) of olive oil over the potatoes. Add salt and toss with your hands until the potatoes are thoroughly coated with oil and salt. Bake for 35 to 40 minutes, stirring once, until golden and can be easily pierced with a fork.

While the potatoes are roasting, combine chipotle pepper, adobo sauce, garlic, lime zest and lime juice in a large bowl.

Once the potatoes are done and still hot, pour them into the chipotle lime dressing. Add cilantro and gently stir to combine, making sure every potato is covered. Plate and serve.

no-churn caramelized white chocolate ice cream

After a night spent over a grill, there's nothing like cold, creamy homemade ice cream—but homemade ice cream involves carefully making a custard and having an ice cream machine. This ridiculously simple recipe uses a well-known no-churn hack and white chocolate that becomes caramelized and nutty when roasted.

serves 8 | prep time: 15 minutes | cook time: 15 minutes

10 oz (283 g) quality white chocolate* (with a 20% or greater cocoa butter)

3⅓ cups (788 ml) heavy cream, divided

½ tsp sea salt

1 (14-oz [385-ml]) can condensed milk

2 tsp (10 ml) vanilla paste or extract

Preheat oven to 260°F (125°C). Chop the chocolate and place on a parchment-lined baking sheet. Roast for 10 to 15 minutes, stirring every 5 minutes, until the chocolate turns golden brown. During roasting the texture might become gritty but will come together at the end. Pour chocolate in a bowl, add ⅓ cup (78 ml) heavy cream, salt and stir until fluid and smooth to make a ganache.

In a blender, food processor or by hand with a whisk, beat the remaining heavy cream until thick and peaks form. In a large bowl, combine condensed milk and vanilla then fold in whipped cream until combined. Pour half of the mixture into a 9 × 5-inch (23 × 13-cm) baking dish and top with half of the roasted white chocolate ganache. Pour the remaining ice cream mixture on top and finish off with ganache. With a bamboo stick or knife swirl the layers together. Cover with parchment or wax paper and freeze for at least 4 hours. Can be made a week in advance.

note

Using a high-quality chocolate is crucial for this recipe, but I have had success using white chocolate chips and adding a tablespoon (15 ml) of a flavorless cooking oil such as canola when roasting to keep the chocolate from separating.

fall

Everyone has a food memory and usually a recipe to go with it. Some of my fondest memories evolved around food. From cooking with those I love to the first memorable flavors of epic meals that took me out of my comfort zone to discover something new, I treasure them all. One such memory was traveling downtown to the farmers' market with my dad to get a pumpkin for my elementary school pumpkin carving contest. Pumpkins of all shapes and sizes were lined up, but I was too distracted by a unique smell to pick one immediately. The cool fall air held the distinct smoky and savory aroma of smoked turkey, and I wasn't leaving the market without some. Thankfully, my dad was on the same page, and there we sat surrounded by hundreds of pumpkins and the hum of the market with turkey legs in our hands. To this day, whenever I smell a smoker going in the brisk breeze, I know it's fall and instantly want to call everyone over for an autumn feast to celebrate the season.

brunch

Persimmon Yogurt

Dutch Baby w/ Pear

Greens, Bacon, & Egg

Toast w/ Sage B

farmers' market brunch

Years ago, we started a tradition that lives to this day: the farmers' market brunch. It began with a group of hungry runners raiding my refrigerator after Saturday morning long runs and leaving my kitchen bare. After a few weekends of waking up and strolling into my kitchen to find this catastrophe, I figured making an event out of it was the only thing to do. So, I put out an open invite for the awesome non-runners (usually friends with kids) to join me at the farmers' market while the crazies went to run around the city. We'd pick up fresh seasonal produce, handmade breads, yogurt, eggs and cheese directly from the market while our kids ran through our feet with glee.

Once we got home, we'd open a bottle of champagne or make Bloody Marys and cook with our newfound goods while the kids played and music filled the house. Yogurts with fruit, crostini with seasonal roasted vegetables, overflowing charcuterie and cheese boards, Dutch baby pancakes and of course, fried farm eggs adorned the table. By the time everyone was done with their run, we'd throw out a stack of plates, make another round of Bloody Marys and it was a party.

Because this is a spur-of-the-moment event, I always rely on simple recipes that can be altered according to the seasonal produce that the market has to offer.

menu

Persimmon Honeyed Yogurt with Toasted Hazelnuts

Dutch Baby with Chai Caramel Pears

Greens, Bacon and Eggs

Toast with Sage Butter

timeline

2 Hours Before—Create Persimmon Honeyed Yogurt, Chai Caramel Pears and Sage Butter / Prepare Ingredients for Greens, Bacon and Eggs

1 Hour Before—Chill Beverages

persimmon honeyed yogurt with toasted hazelnuts

Fresh fall persimmons are a gorgeous fruit with a mild warm sweetness. Here, I've taken plain Greek yogurt, sweetened it with honey and cinnamon and folded it in with sliced persimmons and toasted hazelnuts for a quick fall brunch dish. If persimmons and hazelnuts are unavailable, ripe pears and pecans make a wonderful substitute.

serves 8 | prep time: 10 minutes

½ cup (85 g) hazelnuts

¼ tsp sea salt

32 oz (4 cups [946 ml]) plain Greek yogurt

½ cup (118 ml) honey

2 ripe persimmons, thinly sliced in rounds

Preheat oven to 350°F (175°C). Place hazelnuts on a rimmed baking sheet and toast until golden; about 10 to 15 minutes. Coarsely chop hazelnuts and toss with salt.

In a large bowl, combine yogurt and honey then place into a large serving bowl. Top with sliced persimmons and toasted hazelnuts. Serve.

dutch baby with chai caramel pears

Why a large oven-made pancake is called a Dutch Baby is beyond me, but we simply adore them. A large, airy and thin sweet pancake that takes seconds to prepare might be the perfect brunch food! To take this delicious wonder to the next level, we top it with whatever seasonal fruit we find at the market—in this case pears simmered in brown sugar—and the spices that make up Masala chai.

makes 8 slices | prep time: 15 minutes | cook time: 20 minutes

dutch pancake

3 large eggs

¾ cup (177 ml) whole milk

½ cup (118 g) all-purpose flour

¼ cup (48 g) sugar

1 tsp (5 ml) vanilla paste or extract

¼ tsp salt

3 tbsp (45 g) room temperature butter

chai caramel pears

1 tbsp (15 g) unsalted butter

3 Bartlett pears, cored and diced

2 tbsp (22 g) light brown sugar

2 tbsp (28 g) water

½ tsp ground cinnamon

½ tsp ground cardamom

¼ tsp ground ginger

¼ tsp ground black pepper

⅛ tsp ground clove

Place a 12-inch (31-cm) cast iron skillet in the oven and preheat to 425°F (220°C).

In a blender, combine all ingredients for the Dutch pancake, excluding the butter, and blend on high until frothy, about 30 to 45 seconds.

Add butter to the hot skillet and allow it to melt. Immediately pour the batter into the skillet and bake for 20 minutes or until golden and puffy.

While the pancake is baking, make the pears. In a saucepan, melt butter over medium heat. Once melted, add the remaining ingredients and stir to combine. Simmer for 10 minutes until pears are tender and a "caramel" sauce has formed.

Transfer the Dutch Baby to a serving platter and pour pears on top or serve on the side. Slice into 8 sections and serve immediately.

greens, bacon and eggs

Greens, Bacon and Eggs—my favorite food trifecta and usually abundant at an autumn farmers' market. This simple sauté brings crisp, salty bacon, velvety fall greens and fresh creamy eggs together in a one-pan dish.

serves 8 | prep time: 15 minutes | cook time: 20 minutes

6 slices bacon

1 clove garlic, minced

1 shallot, minced

8 cups (1.5 kg) greens (kale, collard, mustard, chard or spinach) cut into ½-inch (13-mm)-wide ribbons

½ cup (90 g) Parmigiano Reggiano or Pecorino cheese, shredded

1 tsp (5 ml) fresh lemon juice

8 large eggs

Salt and pepper

In a large, heavy skillet over medium-high heat, cook bacon until crisp. Remove bacon to a paper-lined plate and crumble when cooled.

Carefully spoon out about half of the oil leaving about 2 tablespoons (30 ml) of bacon drippings in the skillet. Reduce heat to medium and add garlic and shallots; cook for 2 minutes until fragrant. Add the greens and sauté until just wilted, about 4 minutes. Stir in cheese and lemon juice.

Create 8 wells within the wilted greens. Crack eggs into these wells and cook for about 4 minutes until the whites begin to set. Cover, remove from heat and allow to sit for 4 to 5 minutes until egg whites are cooked through but yolks are still runny. Season eggs with salt and pepper, top with crumbled bacon and serve straight out of the skillet. Serve with buttered toast.

toast with sage butter

There is always a baker selling fresh-baked crusty bread at the farmers' market and I always take advantage of it. There's nothing like fresh bread that's been toasted, slathered with creamy salted butter kissed with a touch of seasonal herbs and served with eggs.

serves 8 | prep time: 5 minutes | cook time: 10 minutes

1 loaf of fresh crusty bread cut into 1-inch (2.5-cm)-thick slices

½ cup (114 g) salted butter, softened

2 tbsp (5 g) chopped fresh sage

Maldon or other flaked sea salt

Place bread on a baking sheet and toast under a low broiler, flipping once, until lightly golden on both sides, about 10 minutes.

In a bowl, combine butter and sage.

Slather bread with sage butter and sprinkle a small pinch of Maldon salt on each slice. Serve with Greens, Bacon and Eggs (page 118).

autumn beer dinner

Thanks to Prince Leopold rolling out the barrels of the good stuff for his nuptial festivities, autumn and beer are forever linked. Those first few days of fall just beg for a tall glass of malty, foamy Oktoberfest or bready, spice-tinged Dunkelweizen. There's more than a little German in our family tree, and we don't hesitate to celebrate our heritage this time of year by putting together a proper beer dinner and hoisting a stein!

We have a select group of craft-beer-obsessed friends and these types of dinner are just for them. Half the fun is handing them the menu for the night with the instructions to bring a bottle that they think would pair with the course. Some are winners and some we laugh about. Either way, a delicious dinner becomes more of an event.

menu

Speck and Mozzarella Crostini with Truffle Oil

Bratwurst and Cabbage with Dunkel Sauce

Slow-Cooker Mashed Potatoes

Vanilla Panna Cotta with Blackstrap Molasses and Graham Crackers

timeline

1 Day in Advance—Create Vanilla Panna Cotta / Prepare Bratwurst for Cooking and Create Dunkel Mustard Sauce / Refrigerate Beer Pairings

Morning of—Create Slow Cooker Mashed Potatoes

1 Hour Before—Prepare Speck and Mozzarella Crostinis for Cooking

30 Minutes Before—Cook Bratwurst

speck and mozzarella crostini with truffle oil

There's a neighborhood pizza shop that serves a thin crust wood-fired pizza that I adore. I crave these flavors so much that I make this appetizer every chance I get. Smoky speck, creamy mozzarella and earthy truffle oil come together on crisp baguette slices for a simple but deep first course.

serves 8 | prep time: 15 minutes | cook time: 10 minutes

1 (16-inch [40-cm]) baguette, sliced into 1-inch (2.5-cm) slices

4 slices speck or prosciutto

8 oz (226 g) fresh mozzarella, sliced into 16 slices

2 tbsp (5 g) fresh sage, thinly sliced

Truffle oil

Flaked sea salt

Preheat oven to 400°F (205°C). Line a baking sheet with parchment paper.

Lay baguette slices on the baking sheet. Cut each slice of speck into four pieces, for a total of 16 slices, and top baguette slices. Next top with mozzarella and bake for 10 to 15 minutes until the crostini is slightly crisp and mozzarella is melted. Remove from oven and garnish with sage, a good drizzle of truffle oil and a pinch of flaked sea salt. Serve.

suggested pairing

Witbier (Belgian Wheat Beer).

bratwurst and cabbage with dunkel sauce

You can never go wrong with the classic bratwurst and beer and this one-pot meal makes for a simple but delicious dinner. The dunkel sauce is a dark German beer sauce flavored with mustard to pair with the bright and tangy cabbage and sausage and can be made in advance and refrigerated until needed.

serves 8 | prep time: 20 minutes | cook time: 50 minutes

bratwurst and cabbage

1 large head red cabbage, shredded

1 bunch small carrots, thinly sliced

½ cup (118 ml) apple cider vinegar

¼ cup (59 ml) water

½ tsp kosher salt

8 pork bratwurst

1 tbsp (14 ml) olive oil

dunkelweizen sauce

2 tbsp (30 g) bacon fat or butter

2 tbsp (15 g) all purpose flour

1 cup (236 ml) Dunkelweizen beer

¾ cup (177 ml) chicken stock

2 tbsp (28 g) whole grain mustard

2 tsp (10 ml) Worcestershire

Pinch salt

Preheat oven to 425°F (220°C).

Place cabbage and carrots in a large roasting pan and add vinegar, water and salt. Lay bratwurst on top of cabbage, drizzle with oil, cover with foil and place in the oven. Braise for 45 minutes, remove foil and braise for an additional 10 minutes.

While brats and cabbage cook, create the Dunkelweizen sauce. In a saucepan over medium heat, heat bacon fat until melted. Add flour and whisk until combined; cook for 2 minutes. Next, add Dunkelweizen, stock, mustard, Worcestershire and salt. Bring to a boil then reduce heat to a simmer. Simmer for 10 to 15 minutes until slightly thickened.

Serve with bratwurst and cabbage over mashed potatoes and drizzle sauce over.

To make in advance, create the sauce a day before and reheat before serving with a little chicken stock if the sauce becomes too thick.

suggested pairing

Anything German! Darker beers are preferred such as Sylvaner and Spatburgunder. If you want wine, try a Riesling.

slow-cooker mashed potatoes

Savory sausage and bright vinegary cabbage with a delicious soulful sauce just screams to be served on a bed of creamy mashed potatoes. So, break out the slow cooker and avoid hovering over a pot of potatoes to make life easier on yourself.

serves 8 | prep time: 15 minutes | cook time: 4 hours

5 lbs (2.3 kg) russet potatoes, peeled and diced

2 cups (472 ml) chicken stock

2 cloves garlic, minced

½ cup (118 ml) whole milk, warmed

½ cup (118 ml) butter, melted

1 tsp (5 g) kosher salt

½ tsp fresh ground black pepper

To the slow cooker, add potatoes, chicken stock and garlic. Cover and cook on high for 4 hours until potatoes are very tender. Turn the heat to warm. With a potato masher or an electric mixer, mash the potatoes until smooth. Add milk, butter, salt and pepper and stir. Add additional milk to reach a smooth consistency, if needed.

Keep covered on warm for up to 2 hours before serving.

vanilla panna cotta with blackstrap molasses and graham crackers

This sweet cream dessert is a grown up version of an ice cream sundae and can be created in minutes and days in advance. It's a fun way to end a dinner and an amazing pairing with a barrel-aged stout.

serves 8 | prep time: 15 minutes | cook time: 5 minutes

1 cup (236 ml) whole milk

1 tbsp (14 g) unflavored gelatin

3 cups (709 ml) heavy cream

⅓ cup (63 g) sugar

2 tsp (10 ml) vanilla paste or extract

⅛ tsp salt

3 tbsp (44 ml) blackstrap molasses

1 tbsp (14 ml) coffee liqueur

½ cup (45 g) graham cracker crumbs

Flaked sea salt

Place milk in a saucepan and sprinkle gelatin over. Allow to stand for 5 minutes until softened. Stir over medium heat until gelatin dissolves, about 5 minutes (do not boil). Add cream, sugar, vanilla and salt. Stir and cook for 2 minutes. Remove from heat and strain into 8 glasses. Refrigerate until set, at least 5 hours and up to 2 days in advance.

When ready to serve, combine molasses and coffee liqueur and spoon over panna cotta. Top each serving with graham cracker crumbs and a pinch of sea salt. Serve.

suggested pairing
Brown Ale or break or bourbon-barrel aged stout.

thanksgiving with friends

I think "Friendsgiving" was a thing on social media for about an hour this year—that's funny to me, because it's something I've been doing since I first left home. We of course do the annual big family feast—ask anyone who marries into my family just how big that gathering can be—but I always make time for a separate celebration for our closest friends.

I never tire of the seasonal flavors of Thanksgiving. Really, I could probably live off of stuffing alone at least one day a week all year! Add in something sweet made with pumpkin, and I'm in fall heaven. This dinner can be as elegant or as casual as you want to make it. I like to make arrangements out of whatever I can find outside at the time; twigs, magnolia leaves or anything natural and rustic.

menu

Bourbon Amaretto Cooler

Dried Cherry and Sage Goat Cheese

Shredded Kale and Brussels Sprouts Salad

Apple and Sausage Stuffing

White Wine Braised Turkey Legs

Pumpkin Pot de Crème with Maple Bourbon Whipped Cream

timeline

2 Days in Advance—Create Pumpkin Pot de Crème

1 Day in Advance—Dry Brine Wine Braised Turkey Legs / Prepare Apple and Sausage Stuffing to be Cooked / Create Dried Cherry and Sage Goat Cheese / Create Maple Bourbon Whipped Cream

Morning of—Bake Stuffing / Prepare Shredded Kale and Brussels Sprouts Salad Keeping Vinaigrette Separate until Serving

1 Hour Before—Braise Turkey / Set Pot de Crème / Set Cheese / Chill Wine

10 Minutes Before—Create Bourbon Amaretto Cooler

bourbon amaretto cooler

This Bourbon Amaretto Cooler is a smooth but refreshing cocktail with a sparkling kick of ginger beer and a touch of lemon—perfect for a small dinner party, or easily doubled for a holiday gathering.

makes 8 (4-oz [113-ml]) cocktails | prep time: 8 minutes

12 oz (355 ml) bourbon whiskey

10 oz (296 ml) ginger beer

6 oz (177 ml) amaretto

4 oz (118 ml) fresh lemon juice

1 tsp (5 ml) orange bitters

Luxardo cherries

In a small pitcher, combine all ingredients and stir.

Serve in lowball glasses over ice and garnish with a Luxardo cherry, if desired.

dried cherry and sage goat cheese

One of the most versatile ingredients, goat cheese is something you can always find in my cheese drawer. This tempting take on the traditional cheese ball infuses tart goat cheese with sweet dried cherries and earthy sage.

serves 8 | prep time: 10 minutes

8 oz (226 g) goat cheese, softened

1 oz (28 g) cream cheese, softened

¼ cup (38 g) dried cherries, chopped

1 tbsp (2.5 g) fresh sage, chopped

1 tbsp (14 ml) cherry preserves

Pinch flaked sea salt

In a bowl, mix together goat cheese, cream cheese, dried cherries and sage.

Place a lightly greased 3-inch (8-cm) round form or biscuit cutter on a serving plate or board and spoon cheese mixture into the form, pack tightly. Remove the form and top cheese with cherry preserves and salt. Serve with crackers.

Can be made two days in advance and stored in the refrigerator. Set cheese out at room temperature and top with cherry preserves prior to serving.

suggested pairing

Sancerre and goat cheese is the classic pairing and will also go beautifully with the following salad. With the cherries and sage added, dry rosé (including sparkling!) comes into play.

shredded kale and brussels sprout salad

This dense salad is full of layers of fresh comforting flavors. Warm walnuts bring a hint of nuttiness to bright green winter vegetables while a red wine vinegar brightens up the whole deal.

serves 8 | prep time: 20 minutes

¾ cup (87 g) walnuts

1 lb (454 g) Brussels sprouts, thinly sliced into ⅛-inch (3-mm)-wide strips

1 lb (454 g) Tuscan kale, thinly sliced into ⅛-inch (3-mm)-wide strips

1 cup (180 g) Pecorino cheese, grated

¼ cup (59 ml) red wine vinegar

2 tbsp (28 ml) Dijon mustard

1 shallot, minced

¼ tsp kosher salt

⅛ tsp freshly ground black pepper

½ cup (118 ml) extra virgin olive oil

In a preheated 350°F (175°F) oven, toast the walnuts until golden and fragrant, about 5 minutes. Remove and cool. Store, covered, at room temperature until use.

In a large bowl, toss to combine Brussels sprouts, kale and cheese. In another bowl, whisk to combine vinegar, mustard, shallot, salt and pepper. While whisking, slowly pour in the olive oil and whisk until emulsified. Both the vinaigrette and salad can be made in advance, stored separately in the refrigerator.

Add the vinaigrette and walnuts to the kale and toss to combine. Serve.

apple and sausage stuffing

My grandmother's classic cornbread stuffing is hard to beat; but when I'm looking for something a little more exciting, I turn to this hearty fall-inspired stuffing using a crusty whole grain loaf of bread studded with nutty seeds and folded with apples, sage and savory pork sausage.

serves 8 | prep time: 20 minutes | cook time: 50 minutes

1 tbsp (15 ml) grapeseed or canola oil

1 lb (454 g) Italian pork bulk sausage

1 cup (151 g) yellow onion, diced

1 cup (151 g) celery, diced

1 cup (180 g) Granny Smith apples, diced

2 garlic cloves, minced

2 cups (472 ml) chicken stock

3 large eggs, beaten

2 tbsp (5 g) fresh sage, chopped

½ tsp kosher salt

¼ tsp fresh ground black pepper

1 lb (454 g) whole grain seeded bread, cubed

4 tbsp (57 g) butter, cubed

In a large sauté pan, heat oil over medium heat. Add sausage and cook until browned, breaking into pieces with a spoon, about 8 to 10 minutes. Remove sausage to a large bowl. Add onion, celery, apples and garlic to the pan and sauté until apples are soft, about 5 minutes, then add to sausage. Add chicken stock, eggs, sage, salt and pepper and stir to combine. Can be made 1 day ahead and stored covered in the refrigerator until needed—allow to sit at room temperature for 30 minutes before cooking.

Preheat oven to 350°F (175°C). Place bread on a baking sheet and toast until slightly golden, about 10 minutes. Add to sausage mixture and fold to coat.

Pour into a buttered 9 × 13-inch (23 × 33-cm) baking dish and equally distribute cubed butter over. Bake, uncovered, for 50 minutes or until cooked through.

white wine braised turkey legs

Everyone fights over the turkey legs, so I never fail with this fool-proof recipe. These fall-off-the-bone tender turkey legs are incredibly simple to make and just require an overnight dry brine (optional but amazing), a quick sear and a few hours in the oven. With delicate flavors of pink peppercorn, coriander and orange zest, this recipe is irresistible.

serves 8 | prep time: 20 minutes | cook time: 2 hours

peppercorn dry brine

1 tbsp (8 g) black peppercorns

1 tbsp (8 g) pink peppercorns

1 tsp (3 g) coriander seeds

2 whole star anise

3 bay leaves

1½ tbsp (22 g) kosher salt

2 tbsp (27 g) brown sugar

1 tbsp (9 g) grated orange zest

turkey legs

2 tbsp (30 ml) grapeseed or canola oil

4 turkey drumsticks

4 turkey thighs

1 leek, sliced in half lengthwise

2 carrots

3 cloves garlic, peeled

2 cups (472 ml) dry white wine

1 cup (236 ml) chicken stock

In a skillet, toast black and pink peppercorns, coriander seeds, anise and bay leaves over medium heat until fragrant, about 3 minutes. Transfer to a coffee grinder or food processor and process until fine. You can alternatively place in a plastic food-safe bag and crush with a mallet or rolling pin until coarse. Combine with salt, sugar and orange zest. Rub mixture over the turkey and place in glass dish and cover with plastic wrap. Refrigerate overnight.

Preheat oven to 325°F (165°C). Rinse the turkey legs completely with water and pat dry with paper towels.

In a roasting pan or large heavy-bottomed pot large enough to hold the turkey, heat oil over high heat. Sear the turkey until golden, about 3 minutes a side. Remove turkey and add leeks, carrots and garlic; sauté for 2 minutes or until lightly browned and remove. Add wine and bring to a boil. Simmer until reduced by half then add the chicken stock, turkey (skin side up) and vegetables; bring to a boil. Immediately cover with foil or lid and place in the oven. Braise for 2 hours, or until the turkey is tender and falling off the bone, then remove the lid and allow to cook for another 15 minutes to allow the skin to slightly crisp.

Strain the pan juices from the vegetables and serve as a sauce alongside the turkey legs.

suggested pairing

Chenin Blanc or Riesling if you want white; keep it dry to off-dry. For reds, Cru Beaujolais (best crus are Fleurie, Morgon, Brouilly, Julienas or Moulin-a-vent), Pinot Noir or Spanish Garnacha are light enough to not overpower. Beer: Saison, Farmhouse, Lager, wheat beers or even a Belgian Wild Ale will pair nicely.

pumpkin pot de crème with maple bourbon whipped cream

An absolute favorite in the fall, Pumpkin Pot de Crème is a deliciously indulgent experience. I love it because it can be made a few days in advance and always is talked about afterwards.

serves 8 | prep time: 15 minutes | cook time: 40 minutes

pot de crème

1½ cups (354 ml) heavy cream

1 cup (236 ml) milk

⅔ cup (157 ml) maple syrup

1 cup (236 ml) pumpkin purée

8 egg yolks

1 tsp (5 ml) vanilla paste or extract

1 tsp (2.5 g) ground cinnamon

½ tsp fresh grated nutmeg

¼ tsp ground ginger

¼ tsp salt

whipped cream

1 cup (236 ml) heavy cream

2 tbsp (10 ml) bourbon

2 tbsp (10 ml) maple syrup

Preheat oven to 350°F (175°C).

In a saucepan over medium heat, combine cream, milk, syrup and pumpkin and stir. Bring to a simmer. Once simmering, remove from heat.

In a medium bowl, whisk to combine egg yolks, vanilla, cinnamon, nutmeg, ginger and salt. Very slowly, in a small stream, pour the pumpkin mixture into the egg mixture while whisking.

Place 8 (4-ounce [118-ml]) ramekins in a roasting pan or oven-safe dish with high sides. Pour the pumpkin filling into each ramekin leaving a ½-inch (13-mm) space at the top. Pour hot water into the roasting pan until the water reaches halfway up the ramekins. Bake for 40 to 45 minutes or until the custard has set but still has a jiggle to it. Cool at room temperature for 10 minutes then carefully remove the ramekins from the water bath. Place in the refrigerator and refrigerate at least 4 hours or overnight. Can be made 2 days in advance.

Place heavy cream, bourbon and maple syrup in a blender. Blend for 40 to 60 seconds or until the cream thickens and does not fall off a spoon when held upside down. Be careful not to over whip. Can be made 1 day in advance.

When ready to serve, spoon a dollop of whipped cream onto each pot de crème and garnish with a pinch of cinnamon.

game day
for food snobs

Our house is packed during college football and hockey season, and we have the smallest TV, so I'm thinking people really just come for the food and to have fun. Whether people gather for your sweet entertainment center or if it's just another reason to get together, game day is the time to pull out all the stops on the comfort food. Nachos, wings, popcorn—just let it all fly!

My game day setup is one of casual convenience where everyone serves themselves. I usually like a mixture of snack foods made in advance and hot food served in stages; one at kickoff, and one at halftime to keep the party alive and going so it doesn't matter if our team is losing.

I keep plenty of options of self-serve refreshments out on the bar: iced tea, lemon water, a large ice bucket full of good beer and my secret stash of bourbon for those who appreciate it.

menu

Curried Snack Mix

Porter-Braised Short Rib Nachos

Brown Sugar Chipotle Wings

Caramelized Onion Dip

Whisky Caramel Brownies

timeline

1 Week in Advance—Create Curried Snack Mix

2 Days in Advance—Prepare Caramelized Onion Dip

1 Day in Advance—Braise Short Ribs and Make Beans / Prepare Whisky Caramel Brownies and Caramel

Morning of—Create Sauce for Brown Sugar and Chipotle Wings

30 Minutes Before—Assemble and Bake Short Rib Nachos

curried snack mix

Snack mix is ubiquitous game day food, but it's also great just to have around the house for a treat or a surprise cocktail party. This snack mix is inspired by an Indian snack called Hot Mix that's composed of nuts, crispy noodles and raisins seasoned with curry. Make it up to a week in advance and store in an airtight container.

makes 9 cups (1,363 g) | prep time: 15 minutes | cook time: 10 minutes

3 cups (64 g) square rice cereal

2 cups (100 g) pretzel sticks

1 cup (60 g) rice crackers

1 cup (60 g) sesame sticks

1 cup (170 g) raw cashews

¼ cup (32 g) raw pumpkin seeds

¼ cup (57 g) unsalted butter

2 tsp (4 g) curry powder

1 tsp (5 ml) soy sauce

1 tsp (4 g) sugar

½ tsp cayenne

¼ tsp salt

½ cup (75 g) golden raisins

Preheat oven to 250°F (120°C).

In a large bowl, combine rice cereal, pretzels, rice crackers, sesame sticks, cashews and pumpkin seeds.

In a saucepot over medium heat, melt butter, curry, soy, sugar, cayenne and salt; stir to combine. Once sugar has melted, pour over mix and toss to coat. Spread evenly on a rimmed baking sheet and bake for 1 hour. Add raisins and cool completely. Store in an airtight container until ready to serve.

porter-braised short rib nachos

Nachos, properly put together, can be the star of any game day feast and these are pretty spectacular. Slow-braised short ribs and black beans can be made up to two days in advance, then thrown together at the last second for an unforgettable pile of nachos perfect for game day.

serves 8 | prep time: 30 minutes | cook time: 2 hours 30 minutes

2 lbs (908 g) bone-in short ribs

1 tsp (5 g) kosher salt

½ tsp fresh ground black pepper

1 tbsp (14 ml) grapeseed or canola oil

12 oz (355 ml) porter beer

1 cup (236 ml) beef stock

2 cloves garlic, peeled and crushed

1 tsp (3 g) espresso powder

1 (15-oz [425-g]) can black beans, drained and rinsed

1 bag corn tortilla chips

1 cup (236 ml) vinegar-based barbecue sauce

2 cups (222 g) Monterey jack cheese, shredded

1 cup (120 g) cheddar cheese shredded

½ cup (75 g) red onion, diced

½ cup (80 g) tomatoes, diced

3 tbsp (7.5 g) cilantro, chopped

1 avocado, diced

½ cup (60 g) queso fresco, crumbled

Preheat oven to 325°F (165°C).

Season short ribs with salt and pepper. In a 6-quart (5.6-L) heavy bottomed pot, heat oil and brown short ribs on all sides. Add porter, stock, garlic and espresso powder. Bring to a boil then remove from heat and place in the oven. Braise for 2 hours and 30 minutes until the meat is falling off the bone. Reserve ½ cup (118 ml) of braising liquid. Allow the ribs to cool then remove the meat and place in an airtight container with ¼ cup (60 ml) of the braising liquid and refrigerate. Place the beans in a blender or food processor with the remaining braising liquid and purée until smooth. Store in the refrigerator until needed. Can be made up to 2 days in advance.

Preheat oven to 350°F (175°C). Line a large baking sheet with foil and arrange ½ of the tortilla chips on the baking sheet. Top with half of the short ribs, beans, sauce and cheeses. Next, add another layer of chips and the remaining short ribs, beans, sauce, cheese and red onion. Place in the oven and bake for 20 minutes until cheese is melted. Top with tomatoes, cilantro, avocado and queso fresco. Serve.

suggested pairing

Darker beers, sangria, Zinfandel, red blends.

caramelized onion dip

Is anyone a fan of "put the powder in the sour cream tub" onion dip? Yecch. One day, however, I happened on a recipe that used caramelized onions and was instantly hooked. Years later, it's still my back-up dip for watching any game from hockey to football. Make a few days in advance and bring it out when guests arrive.

makes 2 cups (400 g) | prep time: 10 minutes | cook time: 30 minutes

2 tbsp (28 ml) olive oil

2 tbsp (30 g) unsalted butter

2 large yellow onions, peeled, halved and thinly sliced

4 oz (113 g) cream cheese

½ cup (118 ml) sour cream

½ cup (118 ml) quality mayonnaise

½ tsp kosher salt

2 tbsp (5 g) fresh chives, chopped

In a large sauté pan over medium heat, combine olive oil and butter. Add onions and sauté for 10 minutes, stirring occasionally. Reduce heat to medium-low and cook for an additional 20 minutes until onions are deep golden and caramelized. Add 2 tablespoons (30 ml) of water and stir, scraping the browned bits off of the bottom of the pan. Cook until water is gone. Season with a pinch of salt and pepper and cool.

With a stand mixer and a paddle attachment or a hand mixer, cream together cream cheese, sour cream and mayonnaise. Add kosher salt, onions and chives and mix to combine. Taste and add additional salt and pepper, if needed. Can be made 3 days in advance and stored in the refrigerator. Serve with chips, crackers and/or vegetables.

brown sugar and chipotle chicken wings

You can't have a game day party without chicken wings, in my opinion. The beauty of these sweet and spicy wings are that they are baked and not fried, saving you an hour sitting in front of the stove, but they are still deliciously crisp. To help with prep time on the big day and to help the wings become extra crispy, place the wings on baking sheets after patting them dry and store in the refrigerator, uncovered, the night before.

serves 8 | prep time: 10 minutes | cook time: 50 minutes

4 lbs (1.8 kg) chicken wings, drumettes and flats separated

¼ cup (59 ml) unsalted butter, melted

2 tbsp (27 g) brown sugar

1 chipotle pepper in adobo sauce, minced

2 tsp (5 ml) adobo sauce

1 tsp (5 ml) apple cider vinegar

½ tsp kosher salt

Place oven racks in the upper and lower positions. Preheat oven to 450°F (235°C).

With paper towels, pat chicken wings dry and divide between two large rimmed baking sheets, being careful not to overlap. Roast for 35 minutes, flip wings and continue to roast for 15 to 20 minutes until golden and crisp.

While the wings are roasting, combine melted butter, brown sugar, chipotle pepper, adobo sauce, vinegar and salt in a large bowl (big enough to hold all the wings). Stir until smooth and sugar has dissolved.

Immediately after the wings come out of the oven, transfer them to the sauce and toss to coat. Plate the wings and serve.

whiskey caramel brownies

These brownies are the cure-all for what ails you. It starts with a simple enough brownie recipe, but then gets turned up to eleven with a luscious whisky caramel sauce! Both of these can be made a day in advance.

makes 12 large brownies | prep time: 30 minutes | cook time: 30 minutes

brownies

½ cup (62 g) all-purpose flour

1½ tsp (5 g) baking powder

1½ cups (270 g) dark chocolate, coarsely chopped

1 cup (170 g) unsweetened chocolate, coarsely chopped

½ lb (227 g) unsalted butter, cut into cubes

3 large eggs

1¼ cups (240 g) sugar

1 tbsp (5 g) espresso powder

1 tbsp (14 ml) pure vanilla extract or paste

caramel

½ cup (95 g) sugar

¼ cup (59 ml) water

½ cup (118 ml) heavy whipping cream

2½ tbsp (37 ml) scotch whisky—use a peaty scotch such as Laphroaig

½ tsp sea salt

Preheat oven to 350°F (175°C). Grease a 9 × 13-inch (23 × 33-cm) baking pan and line with parchment paper with paper hanging off of two opposite ends of the pan.

Whisk the flour and baking powder in a small bowl and set aside.

In a large heatproof bowl, combine 1 cup (180 g) of the chocolate chips and butter. Set it over a pot of simmering water and stir frequently until the chocolate and butter are melted and smooth. Remove from heat. You can alternatively microwave the chocolate and butter in 30-second increments, stirring frequently until melted.

In a medium bowl, whisk eggs, sugar, espresso powder and vanilla until combined.

Add egg mixture to the chocolate mixture and stir until thickened, about 3 to 5 minutes. Add flour mixture to the chocolate and mix until combined. Fold in the remaining chocolate chips.

Pour the batter evenly into the prepared pan. Bake for 25 to 30 minutes. Remove by lifting the brownies out by the parchment paper and allow to cool on a wire rack.

In a small heavy-bottom pot, stir to combine sugar and water for the caramel. Bring to a rapid simmer over medium-high heat. Without stirring, let simmer until the color changes to light brown, about 5 minutes, then turn off heat. Slowly stir in cream, scotch and salt until combined. Set in the refrigerator until thickened, about 5 minutes. Pour caramel over brownies, slice and serve.

winter

In my head, winter has this intense soundtrack of a New Orleans jazz band. There's no story behind it, and I can't explain why, but for months I think to a beat of a brassy trumpet that is very festive and beckons me to entertain. Thankfully, with the winter holidays, there is always an excuse to throw a party and plenty of people around to do so. For me, this is the time of year that I really want to celebrate those closest to me. Whether it is an elegant meal around the table or a cocktail party where every room in the house is filled with chatter, this is the most festive season and the perfect time to enjoy the company of friends, neighbors and family.

wine and dine

Probably my first thought upon being asked to write this book was "Wine dinner!" My husband is in the wine business and is constantly studying for the next sommelier exam, so I'm always being bombarded with "what varietal or region" questions when frankly, I'd sometimes rather just enjoy the glass of wine. However, there's no denying that the perfect pairing is usually right at hand in my house.

There's a lot of talk about food and wine pairings, but it really boils down to this: The dish and the glass should elevate each other—it's not about showing off the geekiest or most expensive thing in your cellar.

Fortunately, it's a big world and there are wines for every palate and budget and lots of room for experimentation. While it helps to know a little about wine and the general classic flavor profiles, if you and your guests like the pairing, then it's a good one. So don't be intimidated—pop a cork and find your favorites. It's a time to explore something new and have fun while doing it. Make sure to have plenty of glasses on hand and serve small pours with each plate.

menu

Bacon-Wrapped Dates with Rosemary Goat Cheese

Chilled Butternut Squash Salad with Roasted Shallot Dressing

Red Wine Braised Leg of Lamb

Make-Ahead Parmesan Risotto

Blue Cheese and Honey

timeline

1 Day in Advance—Prepare Bacon-Wrapped Dates and Refrigerate / Roast Squash and Create Roasted Shallot Dressing / Braise Red Wine Braised Leg of Lamb

Morning of—Prepare Parmesan Risotto

1 Hour Before—Chill Wine / Prepare Ingredients to Finish the Risotto / Assemble the Chilled Butternut Squash Salad

30 Minutes Before—Reheat Lamb

10 Minutes Before—Roast the Dates

bacon-wrapped dates with rosemary goat cheese

Bacon-wrapped dates are a classic sweet and savory combination that excites your senses. We like to add a little rosemary infused goat cheese as an added level of flavor. Prep these a day in advance and bake them right before guests arrive.

makes 24 | prep time: 15 minutes | cook time: 15 minutes

3 oz (85 g) goat cheese

1 tbsp (2.5 g) fresh rosemary, chopped

24 dates, pitted

8 slices bacon, sliced into thirds

Preheat oven to 375°F (190°C) and line a baking sheet with parchment paper.

Combine goat cheese and rosemary.

Slice dates along one side so they open up flat. Stuff with a small spoonful of goat cheese mixture, close, then wrap with a bacon slice; skewer with a toothpick if needed. Place on the baking sheet and bake for 15 to 20 minutes, flipping once, until bacon is cooked and golden. Serve.

suggested pairings

Côtes-du-Rhône or domestic Rhone-style blends.

chilled butternut squash salad with roasted shallot dressing

I adore this salad. With sweet and savory notes of caramelized squash and a unique dressing, it's the perfect way to get the dinner started. The different elements of this salad can be made a day in advance and prepared before serving.

serves 8 | prep time: 20 minutes | cook time: 35 minutes

2 lbs (907 g) butternut squash

1 tbsp (15 ml) grapeseed or canola oil

1 shallot

2 cloves garlic

¼ cup (60 ml) pumpkin seed oil (or grapeseed or canola)

2 tbsp (30 ml) balsamic vinegar

½ tsp Dijon mustard

6 cups (120 g) arugula

½ cup (64 g) roasted and salted pumpkin seeds

Preheat oven to 425°F (220°C).

Microwave whole butternut squash for 1 minute to make peeling and cutting easier. With a vegetable peeler, peel the butternut squash then slice into 1-inch (2.5-cm) cubes, discarding the seeds.

Place butternut squash on a rimmed baking sheet with whole shallot and garlic and toss with the oil and a pinch of kosher salt. Roast for 35 minutes or until fork tender. Allow to cool.

Store squash in an airtight container and refrigerate until needed. With your fingers, gently squeeze shallot and garlic out of their skins and place in a food processor or blender. Add remaining oil, vinegar, mustard and season with a pinch of salt and pepper. Purée until smooth and store in refrigerator until needed.

Before serving, toss chilled butternut squash, arugula, pumpkin seeds and dressing until combined and serve.

suggested pairings
Neutral whites like Pinot Gris from Alsace or for Italy, Soave.

red wine braised leg of lamb

This dish was inspired after spending time in the California raisin fields during a harvest. When I came home I immediately craved the sun-kissed and earthy flavors of dry vegetal wines and deep vivid raisins and quickly paired them with a grassy flavored leg of lamb. It's now one of my most cherished recipes that will convert anyone who claims to not like lamb.

serves 8 | prep time: 30 minutes | cook time: 4 hours

5-lb (2.6-kg) leg of lamb, bone-in

1 tsp (5 g) kosher salt

½ tsp fresh ground black pepper

1 tbsp (15 ml) grapeseed or canola oil

2 cups (472 ml) dry red wine

6 oz (170 g) tomato paste

4 ripe tomatoes, quartered

1 cup (151 g) golden raisins

5 cloves garlic, peeled

6 sprigs fresh thyme, plus more for garnish

3 sprigs fresh oregano

3 sprigs fresh rosemary

1 tbsp (15 g) butter

½ cup (70 g) pine nuts

Preheat oven to 325°F (165°C). Season the leg of lamb with salt and pepper. In a large braising pot, Dutch oven or roasting pan, heat oil on high. Place the seasoned lamb in the pot and sear each side until dark brown, about 3 minutes a side.

Once the lamb is finished browning, turn off heat and add wine, tomato paste, tomatoes, raisins, garlic, thyme, oregano and rosemary. Cover and place in the oven. Cook for 1 hour, then reduce heat to 275°F (135°C) and braise for another 3 hours.

Once the lamb is finished, remove it to a plate and cover it with foil. Using a large strainer, strain the leftover ingredients from the pan juices, return to the pot and bring to a boil. Reduce heat to medium-low and simmer for 15 to 20 minutes until reduced by half. Finish it off by adding butter and stir to combine. Can be made a day in advance. About 30 minutes prior to guests arriving, reheat the lamb with ½ cup (120 ml) water, covered, in a 325°F (165°C) oven. Once warmed through, carve the lamb and keep warm. Reheat sauce on the stove until hot.

Lightly toast the pine nuts in a skillet over medium heat until lightly golden. Serve lamb on top of a serving of risotto and garnish with sauce, a spoonful of toasted pine nuts and thyme leaves.

suggested pairing

Won't be cheap, but good Bordeaux (I love Margaux), Pinot lovers—Chambertin; Italian preference, big Tuscan blends.

make-ahead parmesan risotto

For a long time, I didn't serve risotto when entertaining. Not only did it require standing over a pot stirring for 30 minutes, but if left sitting for longer than 10 minutes it became embarrassingly gummy. Then one day I noticed at one of the restaurants where my husband worked that the risotto was prepared in advance and left partially cooked, waiting on the line in large trays, for an order. So I asked the chef the secret, and now it's risotto for everyone! Creamy, warm and soul-filling on a cold winter night, this cheesy risotto is simply stunning.

serves 8 | prep time: 5 minutes | cook time: 25 minutes

8 cups (1893 ml) chicken stock, warmed

2 tbsp (30 ml) olive oil

1 shallot, minced

1 lb (454 g) carnaroli (preferred) or arborio rice

1 cup (236 ml) chardonnay

1 cup (180 g) Parmigiano-Reggiano

3 tbsp (45 g) unsalted butter

Warm the stock in a pot and keep it on low heat. In a 6-quart (5.6-L) pot or large sauté pan, heat oil over medium heat and sauté shallot for 2 minutes. Add rice and sauté, stirring frequently, until the edges of the rice start to turn translucent and rice becomes fragrant, about 3 minutes. Add wine and simmer until the wine is absorbed completely.

Add 1 cup (236 ml) of stock, stir and simmer until the stock absorbs completely, this should take about 4 minutes (if it is taking longer, slightly increase your heat). Add another cup of stock, stir and simmer until the stock absorbs completely. Repeat this process another 2 times for a total of 4 cups (946 ml) of stock. Transfer the risotto to a rimmed baking sheet and immediately cool in the refrigerator. Once cool, cover with plastic wrap. Can be made a day in advance.

An hour before serving, remove the risotto from the refrigerator to come to room temperature. About 10 minutes before serving (and once you have everything ready to plate for dinner), transfer risotto back into the large pot or sauté pan over medium heat and add 2 cups (473 ml) of warmed stock. Simmer, stirring occasionally, until all stock has absorbed. Taste. If the risotto is al dente with small bite to it, it is finished. Add ½ cup (118 ml) of stock, cheese and butter, and stir to incorporate. Risotto should have the consistency of creamy porridge and should slowly fall when it hits the plate. If the risotto still has a crunch to it and is not finished, add 1 cup (236 ml) of stock along with the butter and cheese and allow to cook for about 4 more minutes until al dente and creamy. Serve immediately with the lamb.

blue cheese and honey

The classic way to end a heavy winter meal with delectable wine pairings is with cheese. Something as simple as a beautiful blue cheese, honey and a dried-fruit-studded crisp paired with an aromatic white wine is a basic combination that will be surprising and impressive.

serves 8 | prep time: 15 minutes

16 oz (454 g) Roquefort cheese

8 tsp (39 ml) clover or wildflower honey

16 dried fruit and nut crisps (I prefer Raincoast Crisps)

Slice the Roquefort into 8 (2-ounce [57-g]) wedges and plate on serving plates. Top cheese with a teaspoon (5 ml) of honey each and add 2 crisps per plate. Serve.

suggested pairings

The classic pairing is Gewurztraminer from Alsace. You can also pair a white dessert wine like Sauternes or one of the many vin de liqueurs of France like Banyuls, Beaumes-de-Venise or ratafia.

mushroom and pancetta tart

orange and olive salad

duck confit with honey glaze

roasted cauliflower and pomegranate farro

pumpkin seed brittle

winter harvest

Obviously, our family's lifestyle revolves around food and drink and to be that involved with these industries, we have to be immersed in how our food is grown. We take pride in making responsible sustainable food choices and eating seasonally as much as possible. In the winter, our gardens are overflowing with delicious greens and winter vegetables; pecans have been shelled from the backyard trees; jewel-like citrus from the Texas valley comes in by the truck load, and a few times during the season we hunt at our family's ranch and keep our freezer full of quality meats for the year. It's this time of year, after the roar of the holidays is over, that I love to have everyone over for an elegant dinner and share what the year's harvest has brought us.

A gorgeous magnolia tree is outside my house and I take advantage of its leaves this time of year for arrangements that I place around the table and the house. Their two-toned leaves are elegant with white tulips in a vase placed at the center of the table. I also find that a large bowl of citrus like Satsuma oranges with their stems and leaves attached or even pomegranates make an impressive decoration for an elegant winter dinner. Throw out a few tea candles and maybe a little acoustic music through the speakers and you're set.

menu

Mushroom and Pancetta Tart

Orange and Olive Salad

Easy Duck Confit with Orange Honey Glaze

Roasted Cauliflower and Pomegranate Farro

Pumpkin Seed Brittle

timeline

2 Days in Advance—Dry Brine Duck Legs / Prepare Pumpkin Seed Brittle

1 Day in Advance—Prepare Mushroom and Pancetta Tart for Baking / Prepare Duck Confit

Morning of—Make Cauliflower Farro

1 Hour Before—Make Orange and Olive Salad / Chill Wine

Right Before—Reheat Duck and Farro

mushroom and pancetta tart

Earthy cremini mushrooms sautéed in the drippings of crisp pancetta, deglazed with red wine and baked on an airy puff pastry with a blanket of Fontina cheese is an incredible way to start a meal. I use a quality, preservative-free store-bought puff pastry when I want to simplify things and prepare the tart the morning before serving so I can cook it right before guests arrive.

serves 6 | prep time: 15 minutes | cook time: 25 minutes

4 oz (113 g) pancetta, thickly cut (about 2 slices)

6 oz (170 g) cremini mushrooms, stems removed and diced

1 shallot, minced

1 garlic clove, minced

¼ cup (59 ml) pinot noir

1 tsp (2.5 g) rosemary

1 puff pastry sheet

½ cup (52 g) Fontina cheese, shredded

1 tbsp (15 ml) extra virgin olive oil

½ tbsp (7 ml) lemon juice

1 cup (40 g) micro greens

Slice pancetta into ¼-inch (6-mm) cubes and place in a skillet over medium-high heat. Cook until golden and crisp; then transfer to a paper towel-lined plate. Reduce heat to medium and add mushrooms, shallot and garlic. Sauté until mushrooms are cooked and fragrant, about 5 minutes. Add wine and cook, stirring frequently, until there isn't any liquid left in the pan. Remove from heat and cool completely. Add pancetta and rosemary to the mushrooms, taste and season with salt and pepper if necessary.

Roll the pastry into a 10 × 13-inch (25 × 33-cm) rectangle and transfer to a parchment paper-lined baking sheet. With a knife, lightly score a 1-inch- (2.5-cm)-wide border around the outside of the tart. This will make the pastry rise and form a crust when baked. Evenly sprinkle cheese inside of the border and top with mushroom and pancetta mixture. Cover with plastic wrap until ready to bake.

Preheat oven to 400°F (205°C) and bake for 20 to 25 minutes until the crust is puffy and golden. In a bowl, whisk together olive oil and lemon juice and toss micro greens until coated. Garnish tart with the micro greens, slice and serve.

suggested pairings
Syrah, Rhone blends, Pinot.

orange and olive salad

This is a surprisingly complex range of winter flavors. A blend of fresh, sweet and salty creates a uniquely enticing bite. I love to watch everyone's faces when I set it down in front of them, that look of, "Are we good enough friends to actually try this?" and then the utter shock that it tastes wonderful. I like to prepare the oranges in the morning and store in the refrigerator to get nice and cold before serving.

serves 6 | prep time: 15 minutes

3 navel oranges, peeled and sliced into rounds

2 blood oranges, peeled and sliced into rounds

1 cup (180 g) oil-cured pitted black olives, roughly chopped

¼ cup (59 ml) extra virgin olive oil

2 tbsp (30 ml) fresh orange juice

½ tsp sugar

Pinch of sea salt

Fennel fronds or chopped parsley for garnish

Plate 3 to 4 orange slices on each plate. Top with a few spoonfuls of chopped olives. Whisk together olive oil, orange juice, sugar and salt and whisk until sugar has dissolved; spoon over each serving. Garnish with fennel fronds or fresh parsley. Serve.

suggested pairings

Verdicchio. Sauvignon Blanc, Gavi.

easy duck confit with orange honey glaze

An arduous, excruciatingly long task that requires vats of hard to find duck fat and a grueling clean up, duck confit is not something one usually wants to make at home. But with a few nontraditional tricks, this tempting classic can be easily created for any occasion. Luxuriously tender duck legs braised in their own fat can be made days in advance, then reheated with a golden honey glaze with notes of orange, cinnamon and star anise for a deliciously elegant winter meal.

serves 6 | prep time: 20 minutes with an 8-hour marinating period | cook time: 4 hours 15 minutes

6 bone-in duck legs

1 tbsp (15 g) kosher salt

1 tsp (5 g) ground black pepper

6 garlic cloves, peeled

2 bay leaves

½ cup (118 ml) water

3 tbsp (44 ml) fresh orange juice

3 tbsp (44 ml) honey

1 tsp (2 g) orange zest, grated

⅛ tsp ground cinnamon

2 star anise pods

Using a knife, score the skin around the end of each duck leg bone right above the knuckle. Rub duck legs with salt and pepper, place in a rimmed dish and cover with plastic wrap. Refrigerate for at least 2 hours or up to 8 hours for best results. Remove from refrigerator 30 minutes prior to braising.

Preheat oven to 250°F (120°C). Rinse the duck under cool water to remove the salt and pat dry. Place the legs skin side down in a large heavy-bottomed braising dish with a lid or a roasting pan. Add garlic, bay leaves and water; cover with lid or tightly with foil. Place in the oven and braise for 2 hours, turn the duck legs skin side up, cover and braise for an additional 2 hours. This can be made up to 2 days in advance and stored in the refrigerator until needed. Reheat in a 350°F (175°C) oven until heated through, about 10 minutes, then follow glazing instructions.

To make the glaze, combine orange juice, honey, orange zest, cinnamon and star anise in a small saucepot. Heat over low heat for 5 minutes until the glaze begins to thicken slightly.

Place duck skin side up on a baking sheet (foil-lined for easy clean up). With a pastry brush or a spoon, evenly coat the duck legs with the glaze (reheat the glaze to loosen it, if needed). Place under a low broiler on the center rack until the skin is a nice golden brown and begins to crisp, about 5 to 10 minutes. Serve on top of a bed of Roasted Cauliflower and Pomegranate Farro (page 181).

suggested pairings

Wine: Pinot Noir, Grenache, Rosé; Beer: Belgian Ales, Hefeweizen.

roasted cauliflower and pomegranate farro

I could eat this dish all winter long! With the nutty flavor of farro combined with caramelized roasted cauliflower, vivid pomegranate and pecans, this dish is ubiquitous in winter at our house. I like to make it a day in advance and then reheat and add the pecans, parsley and pomegranate just before serving.

serves 6 | prep time: 5 minutes | cook time: 35 minutes

1 (2-lb [908-g]) head of cauliflower, cut into florets

1 tbsp (15 ml) grapeseed or canola oil

1 tsp (5 g) kosher salt

4 cups (946 ml) low-sodium chicken stock or water

2 cups (421 g) Italian farro, rinsed

2 tbsp (30 ml) extra virgin olive oil

¾ cup (65 g) pomegranate arils

½ cup (60 g) pecans halves

3 tbsp (7.5 g) parsley, roughly chopped

¼ tsp freshly grated nutmeg

Preheat oven to 425°F (220°C). Place cauliflower on a baking sheet and toss with grapeseed oil and ½ teaspoon salt. Roast for 30 to 35 minutes until tender and slightly caramelized.

In a medium pot, bring chicken stock and ½ teaspoon salt to a boil. Add farro and cook for 15 to 20 minutes until tender, strain if needed.

In a large bowl, stir to combine cauliflower, farro, olive oil, pomegranate arils, pecans, parsley and nutmeg. Taste and season with salt and pepper, if needed. Serve.

pumpkin seed brittle

Sometimes just a bite of something sweet (maybe served with a good cup of coffee) is the perfect ending to a great meal. I adore pumpkin brittle for that exact purpose. It's intensely sweet but nutty and offers that finishing note with ease. Make these tempting treats a week in advance and if there are leftovers, make sure to send a bag home with your guests.

makes 4 cups (719 g) | prep time: 5 minutes | cook time: 10 minutes

1 cup (192 g) sugar

½ cup (118 ml) light corn syrup

3 tbsp (45 ml) water

1 cup (128 g) raw shelled pumpkin seeds

2 tbsp (30 g) unsalted butter

½ tsp kosher salt

1 tsp (5 ml) vanilla paste or extract

¾ tsp baking soda

½ tsp flaked sea salt

Special tools: candy thermometer

Spray a parchment paper-lined baking sheet with cooking oil spray and set aside until needed.

In a medium saucepan over medium heat, bring sugar, corn syrup and water to a boil, stirring until sugar has dissolved. Cook until a candy thermometer registers 290°F (143°C), about 4 minutes.

Stir in pumpkin seeds, butter, kosher salt and cook, stirring often until golden and 305°F (151°C), about 4 to 5 minutes.

Stir in vanilla and baking soda (mixture will bubble), then immediately pour onto prepared sheet. Using a spatula, spread until even, sprinkle with sea salt, then allow to cool. Once cooled, break into pieces and store in an airtight container, layered with wax or parchment paper, for up to 1 week.

the big
holiday gathering

Music wafting through conversations, laughter in the air and the smells of the holiday feast cooking away are my favorite things about Christmas. Growing up was no different, and I can still remember my insanely large family all huddled in the kitchen looming over the glazed ham and trying to steal a piece of pie before the main meal even hit the plates. Being from Texas, our holiday meals typically consisted of glazed ham, collard greens, sweet carrots and fried pies; that is, except for this one time things went horribly wrong and there was frozen lasagna—an event that has haunted my dreams since I was eight years old. No one should ever suffer the fate of a sad freezer-burnt lasagna on Christmas.

These days now that I'm in the kitchen the most on Christmas, I usually start off with an epic cheese and charcuterie board that gets devoured faster than a worm in a chicken yard, or the adored baked Camembert. Then it's on to an easy glazed ham big enough to feed a crowd, rolls, creamed greens, sweet paprika carrots and pie that's all inspired by flavors I grew up with.

As with most dinners, flowers make a nice touch to any table. Think amaryllis, fresh garland, pinecones, white roses, vases filled with cranberries and so forth. For the kids, I like to cover a table with a big sheet of butcher paper and crayons to keep busy hands occupied. When I'm dealing with this big of a crowd, I tend to make it less formal and more of a buffet style with large platters to feed everyone. Of course, a holiday cocktail is a must as well as plenty of selections of wine and beer to fit everyone's tastes. Finally, to tie it all together, I need my favorite Louis Armstrong Christmas record on repeat.

menu

Winter Pimm's Punch

Garlic and Rosemary Baked Camembert

Brown Sugar Glazed Ham

Creamed Parmesan Collard Greens

Smoked Paprika and Maple Carrots

Bourbon Pecan Pie Shortbread

timeline

2 Days in Advance—Make Bourbon Pecan Pie Shortbread

1 Day in Advance—Make Creamed Collard Greens and Maple Smoked Paprika Carrots / Prepare Winter Pimm's Punch

2 Hours Before—Prepare Glazed Ham

30 Minutes Before—Reheat Greens and Carrots and Keep Warm / Bake Rosemary Baked Camembert

winter pimm's punch

Every holiday party should start with a light cocktail to warm everyone up and make the night start off quicker. This light punch is a winter take on the much-loved summer cocktail, the Pimm's Cup, with apple cider, brandy and warm spices.

serves 12

4 cups (946 ml) apple cider

2 cups (473 ml) Pimm's #1

2 cups (473 ml) brandy

1 orange, sliced into rounds

1 (2-inch [5-cm]) piece of ginger, peeled and sliced

3 star anise

2 cinnamon sticks

1 cup (236 ml) club soda

1 apple, cored and sliced

Juice of 1 lemon

In a large container, combine cider, Pimm's, brandy, orange, ginger, star anise and cinnamon; refrigerate overnight.

Before serving, add club soda, apple and lemon juice and serve in a punch bowl or large pitcher. Serve over ice and garnish with an apple or orange slice.

garlic and rosemary baked camembert

Soft and delicately melted Camembert with garlic, rosemary and white wine is an elegant crowd-pleaser. It's hard not to love this gooey deliciousness, and that's why I serve it during a big crowded party. A 9-ounce (255-g) wheel is what you can typically find in the grocery store and will serve about 6 people, so it's best to double up for a large group. Bake these beauties right in the box and serve with toasted baguette slices and sliced pears.

serves 12 | prep time: 8 minutes | cook time: 20 minutes

2 (9-oz [255-g]) Camembert in boxes

4 tbsp (207 ml) white wine

2 garlic cloves, minced

2 tsp (5 g) fresh rosemary

1 tsp (2.5 g) fresh thyme

Flaked sea salt

Preheat oven to 350°F (175°C).

Remove any plastic wrapping from Camembert wheels, line the boxes with 10-inch (25-cm) squares of parchment paper, then place the Camembert back in the boxes. Place boxes on a baking sheet. Score the top of the Camembert in a diamond pattern and top each wheel with 2 tablespoons (30 ml) of wine, 1 clove garlic, 1 teaspoon (2.5 g) rosemary and ½ teaspoon thyme. Bake for 15 to 20 minutes until the Camembert just begins to melt. Top each wheel with a pinch of salt and serve with toasted baguette slices, crackers and sliced pears or grapes.

suggested pairings

Chardonnay or yeasty sparkling wines like Franciacorta.

brown sugar glazed ham

As I always say, when there's a large hungry crowd to serve, keeping it simple is best, and if that means just customizing up a pre-sliced smoked ham with a soulful glaze and letting it warm in the oven while you're enjoying the party, so be it. All this simple recipe involves is creating a glaze and painting it on the gorgeous ham just before it's done. Serve with soft yeast rolls and mustard for the option to make a sandwich.

serves 12 | prep time: 10 minutes | cook time: 1 hour 30 minutes

10-lb (4.5-kg) bone-in, fully cooked, spiral sliced ham

1 cup (220 ml) light brown sugar

⅔ cup (156 ml) apple cider vinegar

2 garlic cloves, minced

1 tsp (5 ml) Dijon mustard

Allow ham to sit at room temperature 30 minutes prior to cooking.

Preheat oven to 325°F (165°C). Place ham in a roasting pan and bake for 1 hour and 10 minutes.

While the ham is baking, make the glaze by combining brown sugar, vinegar, garlic and mustard in a saucepan and simmer over medium heat until it is thick enough to coat the back of a spoon, about 10 minutes. This can be made a few hours in advance and reheated before use.

Pour the glaze over the entire ham and continue to cook for an additional 20 minutes or until the ham reaches an internal temperature of 140°F (60°C). Serve.

suggested pairings

Pinot Noir, Grenache, Beaujolais/Gamay, Lagrein.

creamed parmesan collard greens

My nanny, whom I called RoRo, was more of a family member than anything and was at every holiday gathering when I was a kid. She was known for her cooking, especially her amazing and deeply soulful collard greens. They were so good, in fact, that she grew tired of people asking for the recipe. Every time I make any type of collard greens I can only hope to make them as good as she did.

serves 12 | prep time: 10 minutes | cook time: 20 minutes

1 tsp (5 g) salt

4 bunches collard greens, sliced into 2-inch (5-cm) pieces

5 slices bacon

1 clove garlic, minced

1 shallot, minced

3 tbsp (23 g) all-purpose flour

2 cups (472 ml) chicken stock

2 cups (472 ml) whole milk

½ cup (90 g) Parmesan-Reggiano cheese, grated

½ tbsp (1 g) thyme leaves

Bring a large pot of water to boil and add salt. Boil collard greens for 5 minutes until tender but still bright green. Strain collard greens from water and immediately transfer to a bowl of ice water.

In a large 12-inch (30-cm) sauté pan, cook bacon over medium-high heat until golden and crisp, about 4 minutes a side. Remove bacon to a paper towel-lined plate. Reduce heat to medium and add garlic and shallots; sauté for 2 minutes until fragrant. Add flour, whisk to incorporate and cook for another 2 minutes. While whisking, add chicken stock, milk, cheese and thyme. Bring to a simmer and reduce heat to medium-low. Add collard greens and cook for 10 to 15 minutes until the greens are tender and the sauce has thickened. Taste and add salt and pepper if necessary. Crumble the bacon and place on top of the greens. Serve.

Can be made up to a day in advance and stored in the refrigerator (store the crumbled bacon in an air-tight container in the refrigerator separately). When ready to serve, reheat on the stove until warmed through and re-crisp the bacon in a warm oven before placing on top of the collard greens.

smoked paprika and maple carrots

These smoky sweet treasures are flavored with pure maple syrup and smoked paprika, and simmered in carrot juice for the most intensely carroty side dish that everyone will love. Their intoxicating bright orange color accents the candy-like flavor while the smoky paprika balances everything out.

serves 12 | prep time: 15 minutes | cook time: 15 minutes

2 cups (472 ml) carrot juice

⅓ cup (78 ml) pure maple syrup

1½ tbsp (11 g) smoked paprika

½ tsp kosher salt

3 lbs (1.4 kg) carrots, peeled and cut into 1-inch (2.5-cm) sections

1 tbsp (15 g) unsalted butter

In a large heavy-bottomed pot, combine carrot juice, syrup, paprika, salt and bring to a boil over high heat. Add carrots and reduce heat to a rapid simmer. Simmer for 10 to 15 minutes until carrots are tender but not mushy. Fold in butter and serve.

Can be made a day in advance, stored in the refrigerator and reheated.

bourbon pecan pie shortbread

Pecan pie is at the absolute top of my dessert list. Why would anyone bake a cake if the sweet caramelized greatness of a proper pecan pie were an option? So inspired by my favorite dessert, I like to serve Bourbon Pecan Pie Shortbread squares after a big holiday meal. It's a take on the classic pecan pie with far less fuss. Densely sweet and toasty with the perfect balance of salty and sweet, these amazing bars can be made the day ahead for an easy holiday dessert.

makes 24 | prep time: 15 minutes | cook time: 40 minutes

shortbread

2 cups (250 g) all-purpose flour

½ cup (110 g) light brown sugar

1 tsp (5 g) kosher salt

12 tbsp (1½ sticks [174 g]) unsalted butter, melted

filling

½ cup (110 g) light brown sugar

½ cup (118 ml) pure maple syrup

1 large egg

2 tbsp (30 ml) bourbon

1 tsp (5 ml) vanilla paste or extract

½ tsp kosher salt

8 tbsp (1 stick [114 g]) unsalted butter, melted

2 cups (241 g) chopped pecans

Preheat oven to 350°F (175°C) and grease a 13 × 9-inch (33 × 23-cm) baking pan.

In a food processor or by hand using a fork and a large bowl, combine flour, sugar, salt and butter. Pulse or mix until combined and mixture begins to stick together when pinched. Pour into prepared baking pan and press to form an even crust. Bake for 20 minutes until slightly golden.

In a large bowl, whisk to combine sugar, maple syrup, egg, bourbon, vanilla and salt. Continue to whisk and slowly pour in the melted butter until incorporated. Pour onto the shortbread and spread the mixture with a spatula until it evenly covers the entire shortbread. Top evenly with chopped pecans. Bake for 25 to 30 minutes until the mixture becomes bubbly and has lightly set. Cool completely until fully set, at least 4 hours, then cut into bars.

Can be made up to 2 days in advance.

cocktails and conversation

Whoever invented the cocktail party is a pure genius and should have a statue in every town square. It's the perfect type of gathering where the night flows just as easily as the drinks and laughter, and, with just a little work, the host can enjoy the party as much as the guests. This is my favorite way to entertain because I can splurge on food and create lots of different flavor profiles with the small bites that cocktail parties are famous for.

The traditional cocktail fare is a selection of sweet and savory hors d'oeuvres and typically you can count on guests eating two to three servings of each. I like to send out invites at least two weeks in advance and start to plan a menu that is composed of at least 90 percent of items that can be made in advance. I serve everything on a well laid-out table with plenty of small plates and napkins.

Then, of course, there's the essential part of the cocktail party—the bar. Unless you have an actual bar in your home, setting up a table where people can easily mingle is key. I usually set up a menu of signature drinks with the directions and ingredients needed to make them so I'm not stuck behind the bar all night. Also, make sure there are plenty of beer and wine choices available. For planning purposes, figure on two drinks per person in the first hour and one drink per hour after that.

Finally, setting the scene is just as important as the food and drinks. The day before the party I arrange the house so that guests can easily flow through the designated rooms and chairs are arranged in small clusters if anyone should want to sit and chat. Music helps set the mood and helps everyone relax (not that the cocktails don't help with that). Days in advance, gather a two-hour playlist of music that you believe everyone would enjoy and keep the volume at a manageable level so guests can still talk. I recently went to a cocktail party where one of the guests was asked to "just throw something on from your phone." His choice was some sort of techno/rap hybrid played at full volume. Unless you're in the club, this is equivalent to sending out wedding invitations in Comic Sans typeface—it just doesn't work! Needless to say, the party ended as quickly as it began; the moral is always keep your guests' tastes and comfort in mind.

Cocktail parties generally last from 2 to 3 hours, but if they go overboard—which happens a lot at my house—make sure everyone has a safe ride home (or have plenty of air mattresses ready to go). Rideshare services are a fantastic way to make sure your guests arrive home safe. Some services even offer an event package, where you can pre-purchase rides (in full or offer a discount for your guests) ahead of time and send a code for them to enter when using the app.

(continued)

menu

Champagne Bar

Cheese and Charcuterie Board

Marinated Olives

Roasted Fingerling Potatoes with Caviar and Smoked Salmon

Cardamom and Rose Water Tea Cookies

Orange Scented Palmiers

timeline

1 Day in Advance—Make Marinated Olives, Orange Scented Palmiers and Cardamom and Rose Water Tea Cookies / Set up Tables and Bar

Morning of—Roast Potatoes

1 Hour in Advance—Create Cheese and Charcuterie Board

30 Minutes Before—Chill Champagne in Ice / Warm Olives

10 Minutes Before—Assemble Roasted Fingerling Potatoes

champagne bar

A champagne bar is a great option for a cocktail party because it's festive, popular, can cut down on your liquor budget and is less intimidating for those who don't make cocktails on a regular basis. Besides, it's time for the champagne cocktail to make a comeback!

To create a champagne bar, set a table out in a spot where guests can easily walk around. Place an ice bucket large enough to keep a few champagne bottles cold at a time and plenty of glasses and cocktail napkins. Add an array of champagne cocktail mixers like juice, infused simple syrup and liqueurs; then sugar cubes, bitters and citrus peels. Prosecco, with its hint of sweetness, makes a nice substitution for champagne. Make sure to circle around and refill the champagne as necessary.

Guests can simply make their own cocktails or use a few helpful recipes you've printed out. The options are endless as to what to put out and create, but here is what our cocktail station generally looks like:

juice

Blood Orange

Pomegranate

simple syrup

Combine 2 cups (472ml) water, 1 cup (192 g) sugar and flavoring ingredient. Bring to a boil then cool, remove solids. Store in an airtight bottle in the refrigerator for up to 1 week.

Rosemary Simple Syrup (add 2 sprigs)

Cranberry Simple Syrup (add 1 cup cranberries [99 g] and simmer for 5 minutes)

bitters

Angostura

Citrus

liqueurs

Chambord

Cassis

Limoncello

Gin

Cognac

Dry Curaçao

cocktail options

winter champagne cocktail
½ oz (15 ml) Cognac + ½ oz (15 ml) Dry Curaçao + ½ oz (15 ml) Cranberry Syrup + 3 oz (89 ml) Champagne

french 75
Sugar Cube +1 oz (30 ml) Gin + 4 oz (118 ml) Champagne + Lemon Peel

blood orange 75
1 oz (30 ml) Gin + ½ oz (15 ml) Rosemary Syrup + 1 oz (30 ml) Blood Orange Juice + 2 oz (60 ml) Champagne

limoncello sparkler
1 oz (30 ml) Limoncello + 3 oz (90 ml) Champagne + 3 Dashes Citrus Bitters

cheese and charcuterie board

If there is one thing I rely on at a party, it's my boards! They're easy, impressive, can feed a very large number of people and cover all the basic flavor groups. You can separate the charcuterie and cheese to two separate platters or arrange on one gigantic board for an exquisite set up. The purpose of a board is to showcase many different options with flavor pairings to please everyone. Basically, it's a large board of fabulous food and can be customized according to what is available to you. Rely on your deli and cheese shop to do all the heavy work for you—all you need to do is put it together. Here are options based on widely available cured meats and cheeses.

serves 10 | prep time: 30 minutes

cheese

10 oz (283 g) aged cheddar, thinly sliced

1 Red Delicious apple, sliced

7 oz (198 g) quince paste, sliced thinly

10 oz (283 g) Manchego, rind removed and thinly sliced in triangles

½ cup (42 g) salted Marcona almonds

¼ cup (59 ml) pesto

10 oz (283 g) brie or soft-ripened triple-cream cheese

1 tbsp (15 ml) wildflower honey

8 oz (226 g) Gorgonzola

¼ cup (21 g) pecans or walnuts

1 sliced Bartlett pear

charcuterie

Coppa (cured pork shoulder), 20 thin slices

Casalingo (cured sausage), 20 thin slices

Rosetta de Lyon (cured sausage), 20 thin slices

Pickled vegetables such as green beans, carrots, okra, olives and gherkins

Whole-grain mustard

Chicken or duck Pâté, sliced 1½ inch (4 cm) thick

Cherry preserves

Variety of crackers and a sliced baguette

Start with the cheeses. Place cheese in varying spots around the board. Next to the cheddar place the apple to pair. Place the quince paste on top or next to the Manchego and place almonds near as well. Decoratively pour the pesto on top of the brie and serve with a knife. Pour the honey over the gorgonzola and place the walnuts and pear next to it.

For the charcuterie, place the charcuterie on the board in between the cheeses with pickled vegetables and mustard. Add the pâté to the board and serve next to the cherry preserves.

Serve with a variety of crackers such as water crackers and crisps (I like the Raincoast brand) and a sliced baguette.

suggested pairings
Anything you like, possibly excepting heavy reds. We always start with bubbles or a crisp French white!

marinated olives

If you're a betting person, put your money down that you will always find olives in my house. When unexpected company arrives or I need an easy appetizer that looks like I put a lot of thought into, this recipe is what I rely on. Perfect for a cocktail party, an intimate dinner or a large gathering, these irresistible olives infused with herbs, garlic and citrus are a quick and easy appetizer. Use unpitted olives for the freshest results and make sure to serve with a small plate or bowl for guests to discard the pits.

makes 2 cups (360 g) | prep time: 3 minutes | cook time: 10 minutes

1 cup (236 ml) extra virgin olive oil

2 strips orange zest (use a vegetable peeler for best results)

2 strips lemon zest (use a vegetable peeler for best results)

4 garlic cloves, peel removed

3 sprigs thyme

1 small sprig rosemary

2 cups (360 g) mixed unpitted brine-cured olives

In a small saucepot over medium-low heat, combine the oil, orange zest, lemon zest, garlic, thyme and rosemary. Bring to a low simmer for 5 minutes or until the garlic becomes fragrant. If the oil begins to bubble too rapidly reduce heat to low to avoid the garlic turning brown.

Add olives and heat for an additional 5 minutes until the olives are warmed through.

Best when served warm or at room temperature.

roasted fingerling potatoes with caviar and smoked salmon

Going old school is always a good thing, and when I'm in a mood for a throwback cocktail party the first thing I want is caviar. This classic recipe is reminiscent of the era glorified by *Mad Men* when martinis flowed like water, Sinatra ruled Vegas and you could light up a cigar anywhere you pleased.

serves 10 | prep time: 20 minutes | cook time: 40 minutes

12 fingerling potatoes, sliced in half lengthwise

1 tbsp (15 ml) grapeseed or canola oil

½ tbsp (2.5 g) fresh rosemary, chopped

½ cup (118 ml) crème fraîche or sour cream

2 oz (56 g) thinly sliced smoked salmon

12 tsp (38 g) chilled caviar or salmon roe

1 tbsp (5 g) fresh parsley, chopped

Fresh ground black pepper

Preheat oven to 400°F (205°C). With a paring knife, carefully shave a small portion of the bottom of the potatoes so they will lay flat and not tip over. Toss potatoes in oil and rosemary and place on a parchment paper-lined baking sheet. Roast for 40 minutes or until easily pierced by a fork. Set aside to come to room temperature. Can be made 1 day in advance and reheated to warm/room temperature.

Just before serving, place a small spoonful of crème fraîche on each potato. Top half of the potatoes with a slice of salmon and the other with a teaspoon (3 g) of caviar. Garnish with parsley and season with a pinch of black pepper.

cardamom and rose water tea cookies

These cookies are a staple in the winter for us. I give them out as gifts and serve them at parties and they have always met with high praise. Incredibly simple to make, these tea cookies are delicately flavored with cardamom and rose water for a truly unique taste. You can find rose water online or at specialty markets.

makes 20 | prep time: 30 minutes | cook time: 35 minutes

1 cup (125 g) all-purpose flour

1½ cups (174 g) walnuts, finely chopped (the smaller the better)

3 tbsp (36 g) sugar

¾ tsp cardamom

½ tsp vanilla extract or paste

2½ tsp (12 ml) rose water

½ cup (1 stick [114 g]) butter, room temperature

1 cup (130 g) powdered sugar

Preheat oven to 300°F (150°C). In a large bowl, combine flour, walnuts, sugar and cardamom. Add the vanilla extract, rose water and butter in small pieces. With your hands, combine everything together until it resembles a coarse meal.

Form the dough into 1-inch (2.5-cm) balls by gently squeezing the dough together and rolling it between your hands. Place the dough balls on a cookie sheet lined with parchment paper. Next, place the cookie sheet in the oven and bake for 35 minutes. Once the cookies are finished baking, carefully transfer to a cooling rack to cool slightly.

Place the powdered sugar on a plate for rolling. Once the cookies have cooled but are still warm to the touch, roll the cookies in the sugar until evenly coated. Return the cookies to the cooling rack and allow to cool completely. Once the cookies have cooled completely, roll them once again in the powdered sugar for a second coat. Store in an airtight container at room temperature until serving. Can be made 2 days in advance.

orange scented palmiers

As a kid, I remember walking into our favorite French bakery and eyeing the gigantic, larger-than-life palmiers. Flaky, sweet and crunchy, I craved those delicately delicious cookies. These days they are my go-to recipe when I need a quick cookie for a party or for a hostess gift, as they can be made with store-bought puff pastry and created in minutes—no stirring required. Although I prefer making my own puff pastry, sometimes that's not an option. For the best palmiers, especially if you are making them in advance and want to avoid that hydrogenated oil taste, purchase quality puff pastry (I prefer Dufour) in specialty stores.

makes 20 | prep time: 10 minutes | cook time: 20 minutes

1 cup (192 g) sugar

1 tbsp (9.5 g) orange zest, grated

⅛ tsp salt

1 sheet quality puff pastry, thawed

Preheat oven to 425°F (220°C). Line a baking sheet with parchment paper.

Combine sugar, zest and salt. Sprinkle half of the sugar mixture on a clean work surface and place puff pastry on top. Evenly sprinkle the remaining sugar on top of the pastry. Using a rolling pin, roll the dough until it is a 13-inch (33-cm) square and the sugar is pressed into the pastry.

Fold the top side of the pastry so it meets halfway to the middle (basically a quarter fold) then fold again to reach the middle of the pastry. Repeat with the bottom half. Then fold one half on to the other half as if closing a book. Slice the pastry into ¼-inch (6-mm) slices and lay flat, cut side up, onto the prepared baking sheet.

Bake for 20 minutes or until golden, flipping halfway through. Cool completely before serving. Can be made in advance and stored in an airtight container at room temperature up to 1 day in advance.

resources

invitations

Paperless Post
Uniquely designed print and online invitations.
PaperlessPost.com

décor and serving

Ebay
Vintage finds, serveware and equipment
Ebay.com

West Elm
Tableware, glassware and textiles
WestElm.com

World Market
Tableware
WorldMarket.com

Anthropologie
Tableware
Anthropologie.com

kitchenware

Le Creuset
French ovens and roasting pans
Cookware.lecreuset.com

Lodge Manufacturing Company
Cast Iron Pans
Lodgemfg.com

John Boos
Cutting/Charcuterie Boards
Johnboos.com

gourmet finds and specialty stores

Drifters Fish
Wild Copper River Salmon
DriftersFish.com

Dufour
Puff Pastry
Dufourpastrykitchens.com

igourmet
Specialty goods: quince paste, flaked sea salt
igourmet.com

Lesley Stowe Fine Foods
Raincoast Crisps
Lesleystowe.com

Scrappy's Bitters
Handcrafted bitters
Scrappysbitters.com

Pink House Alchemy
Handcrafted bitters and syrups
PinkHouseAlchemy.com

Salem Baking Co.
Meyer Lemon Cookies
SalemBaking.com

acknowledgments

Many thanks to:

First of all, I owe an unfathomable thanks to my mother who is an unwavering force of support. From being an amazing grandmother to a cheerleader to an emergency sous chef, thank you from the bottom of my heart for everything you do.

My impatient husband who has pushed me to follow my heart in every way and the unwavering love of my daughter who sees fit to throw out an inspirational quote from a Taylor Swift song or a cat poster—I can never tell which one—whenever I feel stressed. Thank you for your boundless love and teaching me to never give up.

My ridiculously large and amazing family who have provided me with enough stories for a lifetime to write about.

Paula Jones for being an amazing sous chef during this book and a fabulous friend.

My dear friends for your support, love and for eating everything I put in front of you even when it's goat cheese.

Page Street Publishing for seeing something promising in me.

The amazing chefs and photographers who have inspired me from the time before I even knew this is what I wanted to do.

The readers of Steele House Kitchen who have encouraged me and kept me going through all of these years.

The clients of MBS Recipe Development, I wake up every morning deliriously happy and thankful that I have this career because of you.

Much love to you all.

about the author

Meredith Steele is a professional recipe developer, food writer, food photographer and founder of Steele House Kitchen, an acknowledged food blog celebrating creative and fresh foods. Her recipe development and photography company, MBS Recipe Development, specializes in multimedia recipe development for commercial and small business whose clients include everyone from large PR firms to small family wineries. Meredith's work has been published online, in various print media and has been nominated for the *Saveur* Food Blog Awards. She has also written and developed for many food-based websites including JamieOliver.com. When Meredith is not in the kitchen, she's roaming Dallas, Texas with her husband, curly-headed pixie of a daughter and big floppy-eared dog.

index

a

Albariños
  with Blistered Shishito Peppers with Sea Salt and Fish Sauce, 100
  with Roasted Chicken with Fennel and Leek Croutons, 56
American pale ales with Seafood Boil, 68
appetizers
  Blue Cheese and Honey, 170, *171*
  Chilled Shrimp with Cilantro Crème Fraîche, *42*, 43
  Chive Deviled Eggs, *30*, 31
  Chorizo Gougéres, 88, *89*
  Garlic and Rosemary Baked Camembert, *188*, 189
  Herbed Feta Dip, 28, *29*
  Jamón Serrano Manchego Wraps with Quince Paste, 18, *19*
  Marinated Olives, 204, *205*
  Speck and Mozzarella Crostini with Truffle Oil, 124, *125*
Apple and Sausage Stuffing, *140*, 141
Apricot Curry Chicken Sandwiches, *46*, 47
Apricot Curry Glaze, *46*, 47
Apricots, Chardonnay Poached, *58*, 59

asparagus
  Asparagus, Green Onion and Feta Frittata, 22, *23*
  Shaved Asparagus Salad, 32, *33*
Autumn Beer Dinner recipes
  Bratwurst and Cabbage with Dunkel Sauce, *126*, 127
  Slow-Cooker Mashed Potatoes, 128, *129*
  Speck and Mozzarella Crostini with Truffle Oil, 124, *125*
  Vanilla Panna Cotta with Blackstrap Molasses and Graham Crackers, 130, *131*
avocados
  Grilled Flat Iron with Pineapple and Avocado Relish, 104
  Tomatillo and Avocado Salsa, *80*, 81

b

Bacon-Wrapped Dates with Rosemary Goat Cheese, 162, *163*
Barbera wine, with Rosemary Garlic Pork Loin with Fingerling Potatoes, *34*, 35
Beaujolais/Gamay with Brown Sugar Glazed Ham, 190
Bee's Knees Cocktail with Thyme Honey, 40, *41*

beer. *See also* cocktails; drinks; wines; *individual names of beers and wines*
  in Dunkelwiezen Sauce, 127
  in Beer-Braised Carnitas, 82, *83*
  in IPA Quick-Pickle Green Beans, 64, *65*
  in Porter-Braised Short Rib Nachos, *150*, 151
Beer-Braised Carnitas, 82, *83*
Belgian ales
  with Easy Duck Confit with Orange Honey Glaze, 178, *179*
  with 10-Minute Garlic and Rosemary Roasted Salmon, 92, *93*
Belgian Wild Ale with White Wine Braised Turkey Legs, 142, *143*
berries
  Cranberry Simple Syrup, 201
  Black Pepper–Balsamic Strawberries, *20*, 21
Big Holiday Gathering recipes
  Bourbon Pecan Pie Shortbread, *196*, 197
  Brown Sugar Glazed Ham, 190, *191*
  Creamed Parmesan Collard Greens, *192*, 193

Garlic and Rosemary Baked Camembert, *188,* 189

Smoked Paprika and Maple Carrots, 194, *195*

Winter Pimm's Punch, 186, *187*

Black Pepper–Balsamic Strawberries, *20,* 21

Blistered Shishito Peppers with Sea Salt and Fish Sauce, 100–101

Blue Cheese and Honey, 170, *171*

Bordeaux with Red Wine Braised Leg of Lamb, 166, *167*

Bourbon Amaretto Cooler, 134, *135*

Bourbon Pecan Pie Shortbread, *196,* 197

Bratwurst and Cabbage with Dunkel Sauce, *126,* 127

Brown Sugar and Chipotle Chicken Wings, *154,* 155

Brown Sugar Glazed Ham, 190, *191*

Brownies, Whisky Caramel, 156, *156*

Brunch recipes

    Asparagus, Green Onion and Feta Frittata, 22 *23*

    Black Pepper-Balsamic Strawberries, *20,* 21

    Jamón Serrano Manchego Wraps with Quince Paste, 18, *19*

    Overnight Croissant French Toast Bake with Coffee Rum Sauce, *24,* 25

Brussels Sprouts Salad, with Shredded Kale, 138, *139*

Burrata, and Heirloom Tomatoes, *102,* 103

Butternut Squash Salad with Roasted Shallot Dressing, *164,* 165

C

Cabbage, and Bratwurst with Dunkel Mustard Sauce, *126,* 127

California Common beer with Seafood Boil, 68

Caramelized Onion Dip, 152, *153*

Cardamom and Rose Water Tea Cookies, 208, *209*

Carrot Ginger Soup with Mint Cashew Pesto, *54,* 55

Carrots, Smoked Paprika and Maple, 194, *195*

Cauliflower, Roasted, and Pomegranate Farro, *180,* 181

Cava with Seafood Boil, 68, *69*

Chambertin with Red Wine Braised Leg of Lamb, 166, *167*

Champagne Bar, 201. *See also* beer; cocktails; drinks; *individual names of beers and wines*

Champagne with Chive Deviled Eggs, 31

Charcuterie Board, Cheese and, *202,* 203

Chardonnay

    with Apricot Curry Chicken Sandwiches, *46,* 47

    with Carrot Ginger Soup with Mint Cashew Pesto, *54,* 55

    with Garlic and Rosemary Baked Camembert, *188,* 189

Chardonnay Poached Apricots, *58,* 59

cheese

    Bacon-Wrapped Dates with Rosemary Goat Cheese, 162, *162*

    Blue Cheese and Honey, 170, *171*

    Cheese and Charcuterie Board, *202,* 203

    Dried Cherry and Sage Goat Cheese, *136,* 137

    Garlic and Rosemary Baked Camembert, *188,* 189

    Creamed Parmesan Collard Greens, *192,* 193

    Heirloom Tomatoes and Burrata, *102,* 103

    Manchego, 18

    Speck and Mozzarella Crostini with Truffle Oil, 124, *125*

Cheese and Charcuterie Board, *202,* 203

Chenin Blanc with White Wine Braised Turkey Legs, 142, *143*

chicken

    Apricot Curry Chicken Sandwiches, *46,* 47

    Brown Sugar and Chipotle Chicken Wings, *154,* 155

    Roasted Chicken with Fennel and Leek Croutons, 56, *57*

Chilled Shrimp with Cilantro Crème Fraîche, *42,* 43

Chipotle Roasted Potatoes, *106,* 107

Chive Deviled Eggs, *30,* 31

Chorizo Gougéres, 88, *89*

Cilantro Crème Fraîche, *42,* 43

Coconut Curry Mussels, 52, *53*

cocktails. *See also* beer; Champagne Bar; drinks; *individual names of beers and wines*

    Bee's Knees Cocktail with Thyme Honey, 40, *41*

    Winter Pimm's Punch, 186

Cocktails and Conversation recipes

    Cardamom and Rose Water Tea Cookies, 208, *209*

    Champagne Bar, 201

    Cheese and Charcuterie Board, *202,* 203

    Marinated Olives, 204, *205*

    Orange Scented Palmiers, *210,* 211

    Roasted Fingerling Potatoes with Caviar and Smoked Salmon, *206,* 207

Coffee Rum Sauce, 25

cookies. *See also* desserts

    Cardamom and Rose Water Tea Cookies, 208, *209*

    Orange Cardamom Cookies, 36, *37*

    Orange Scented Palmiers, *210,* 211

    Pumpkin Seed Brittle, 182, *183*

Côtes du Rhône with Bacon-Wrapped Dates with Rosemary Goat Cheese, 162

Creamed Parmesan Collard Greens, *192,* 193

Cru Beaujolais with White Wine Braised Turkey Legs, 142

Curried Snack Mix, 148, *149*

d

Demi-sec, with Lemon Elderflower Icebox Cakes, 48

desserts. *See also* cookies

    Bourbon Pecan Pie Shortbread, *196,* 197

    Chardonnay Poached Apricots, *58,* 59

    Lemon Elderflower Icebox Cakes, 48, *49*

    Mango Granita with Honeyed Buttermilk, *84,* 85

    No-Churn Caramelized White Chocolate Ice Cream, 108, *109*

    Persimmon Honeyed Yogurt with Toasted Hazelnuts, 114, *115*

    Pumpkin Pot de Crème with Maple Bourbon Whipped Cream, *144,* 145

    Pumpkin Seed Brittle, 182, *183*

    Sorbet and Prosecco, *70,* 71

    Vanilla Bean and Bourbon Peaches, 96, *97*

    Vanilla Panna Cotta with Blackstrap Molasses and Graham Crackers, 130, *131*

Whisky Caramel Brownies, 156, *156*

Dinner recipes

    Carrot Ginger Soup with Mint Cashew Pesto, *54,* 55

    Chardonnay Poached Apricots, 58, *59*

    Coconut Curry Mussels, 52, *53*

    Roasted Chicken with Fennel and Leek Croutons, 56, *57*

dips

    Caramelized Onion Dip, 152, *153*

    Herbed Feta Dip, 28, *29*

dressings

    chipotle lime dressing, 107

    Roasted Shallot Dressing, 165

Dried Cherry and Sage Goat Cheese, *136,* 137

drinks. *See also* beer; Champagne Bar; cocktails; *individual names of beers and wines*

    Bourbon Amaretto Cooler, 134, *135*

    Mango Granita with Honeyed Buttermilk, 85

    Smoked Sea Salt Mescal Margaritas, 74

    Winter Pimm's Punch, 186, *187*

Easy Duck Confit, Easy, with Orange Honey Glaze, 178, *179*

Dunkelweizen Sauce, for Bratwurst and

Cabbage, *126,* 127

Dutch Baby with Chai Caramel Pears, *116,* 117

e

Easter Lunch recipes

 Chive Deviled Eggs, *30,* 31

 Herbed Feta Dip, 28, *29*

 Orange Cardamom Cookies, 36, *37*

 Rosemary Garlic Pork Loin with Fingerling Potatoes, *34,* 35

 Shaved Asparagus Salad, 32, *33*

Easy Duck Confit with Orange Honey Glaze, 178, *179*

eggs

 Asparagus, Green Onion and Feta Frittata, 22 *23*

 Chive Deviled Eggs, *30,* 31

 Greens, Bacon and Eggs, 118, *119*

 Overnight Croissant French Toast Bake with Coffee Rum Sauce, *24,* 25

f

Farmers' Market Brunch recipes

 Dutch Baby with Chai Caramel Pears, *116,* 117

 Greens, Bacon and Eggs, 118, *119*

 Persimmon Honeyed Yogurt with Toasted Hazelnuts, 114, *115*

 Toast with Sage Butter, *120,* 121

farmhouse ale with White Wine Braised Turkey Legs, 142, *143*

Fava Bean and Cucumber Salad, 44, *45*

Fennel Bread, *66, 67*

feta cheese

 Asparagus, Green Onion and Feta Frittata, 22 *23*

 Herbed Feta Dip, 28, *29*

Fiesta Taco Bar recipes

 Tomatillo and Avocado Salsa, *80,* 81

 Beer-Braised Carnitas, 82, *83*

 Mango Granita with Honeyed Buttermilk, *84,* 85

 Oven Elotes, *76,* 77

 Quick-Pickled Onions, 78, *79*

 Smoked Sea Salt Mescal Margaritas, 74, *75*

Franciacorta

 with Garlic and Rosemary Baked Camembert, *188,* 189

Frascati

 with Heirloom Tomatoes and Burrata, *102,* 103

French toast bake, *24,* 25

Frittata, Feta, and Asparagus and Green Onion, 22, *23*

fruit

 Apricot Curry Chicken Sandwiches, *46,* 47

Chardonnay Poached Apricots, *58,* 59

Dutch Baby with Chai Caramel Pears, *116,* 117

Persimmon Honeyed Yogurt with Toasted Hazelnuts, 114, *115*

Vanilla Bean and Bourbon Peaches, 96, *97*

g

Gamay with Rosemary Garlic Pork Loin with Fingerling Potatoes, *34,* 35

Game Day for Food Snobs recipes

 Brown Sugar and Chipotle Chicken Wings, *154,* 155

 Caramelized Onion Dip, 152, *153*

 Curried Snack Mix, 148, *149*

 Porter-Braised Short Rib Nachos, *150,* 151

 Whisky Caramel Brownies, 156, *156*

Garlic and Rosemary Baked Camembert, *188,* 189

Garnacha with White Wine Braised Turkey Legs, 142, *143*

Gavi with Orange and Olive Salad, *176,* 177

Gazpacho with Lobster Relish, *90,* 91

Gose beer

 with Chilled Shrimp with Cilantro Crème Fraîche, *42,* 43

with Blistered Shishito Peppers with Sea Salt and Fish Sauce, 100–101

green beans

IPA Quick-Pickle Green Beans, 64, *65*

Sautéed Green Beans with Miso-Mustard Vinaigrette, *94,* 95

Grenache

with Brown Sugar Glazed Ham, 190

with Easy Duck Confit with Orange Honey Glaze, 178

Grilled Flat Iron Steak with Pineapple-Avocado Salsa, 104, *105*

Grillo with Chilled Shrimp with Cilantro Crème Fraîche, 43

Gruno Veltliner with Asparagus, Green Onion, and Feta Frittata, 22

h

Ham, Brown Sugar Glazed, 190, *191*

Hefeweizers with Easy Duck Confit with Orange Honey Glaze, 178

Heirloom Tomatoes and Burrata, *102,* 103

Herbed Feta Dip, 28, *29*

holiday recipes. *See* Big Holiday Gathering recipes

i

Ice Cream, No-Churn Caramelized White Chocolate, 108, *109*

Indian Summer Cookout recipes

Blistered Shishito Peppers with Sea Salt and Fish Sauce, 100, *101*

Chipotle Roasted Potatoes, *106,* 107

Grilled Flat Iron with Pineapple-Avocado Salsa, 104, *105*

Heirloom Tomatoes and Burrata, *102,* 103

No-Churn Caramelized White Chocolate Ice Cream, 108, *109*

IPA Quick-Pickle Green Beans, 64, *65*

j

Jamón Serrano Manchego Wraps with Quince Paste, 18, *19*

k

Kabinett Riesling with Herbed Feta Dip, 28, *29*

l

Lagrein

with Brown Sugar Glazed Ham, 190

with Rosemary Garlic Pork Loin with Fingerling Potatoes, *34,* 35

Leg of Lamb, Red Wine Braised, 166, *167*

Lemon Elderflower Icebox Cakes, 48, *49*

Lobster Relish, and Gazpacho, *90,* 91

m

Make-Ahead Parmesan Risotto, *168,* 169

Malbec with Beer-Braised Carnitas, 82, *83*

Mango Granita with Honeyed Buttermilk, *84,* 85

Manzanilla sherry with Chorizo Gougéres, 88, *89*

margaritas

with Beer-Braised Carnitas, 82, *83*

Smoked Sea Salt Mescal Margaritas, 74

Marinated Olives, 204, *205*

Mayonnaise, Sriracha, 47

Mint Cashew Pesto, with Carrot Ginger Soup, *54,* 55

Miso-Mustard Vinaigrette, 95

Muscadet with Seafood Boil, 68, *69*

Mushroom and Pancetta Tart, 174, *175*

Mussels, Coconut Curry, 52, *53*

n

Nachos, Porter-Braised Short Rib, *150,* 151

No-Churn Caramelized White Chocolate Ice Cream, 108, *109*

O

Olives, Marinated, 204, *205*

Onions, Caramelized, Dip, 152, *153*

Orange and Olive Salad, *176*, 177

Orange Cardamom Cookies, 36, *37*

Orange Scented Palmiers, *210*, 211

Oven Elotes, *76*, 77

Overnight Croissant French Toast Bake with Coffee Rum Sauce, *24*, 25

P

Palo Cortado sherry with Chorizo Gougéres, 88, *89*

Palmiers, Orange Scented, *210*, 211

Pancetta, Mushroom and, Tart, 174, *175*

Party recipes

    Apricot Curry Chicken Sandwiches, *46*, 47

    Bee's Knees Cocktail with Thyme Honey, 40, *41*

    Chilled Shrimp with Cilantro Crème Fraîche, *42*, 43

    Fava Bean and Cucumber Salad, 44, *45*

    Lemon Elderflower Icebox Cakes, 48, *49*

Pecan Pie Shortbread, Bourbon, *196*, 197

Peppercorn Dry Brine, 142

Peppers, Blistered Shishito, with Sea Salt and Fish Sauce, 100–101

Persimmon Honeyed Yogurt with Toasted Hazelnuts, 114, *115*

Pesto, Mint Cashew, with Carrot Ginger Soup, *54*, 55

pickling, quick

    green beans, 64, *65*

    onions, 78, 79

    slaw, 47

Pilsner beer

    with Chilled Shrimp with Cilantro Crème Fraîche, 43

    with Seafood Boil, 68

Pineapple-Avocado Salsa, and Grilled Flat Iron, 104, *105*

Pinot with Mushroom and Pancetta Tart, 174, *175*

Pinot Bianco and Pinot Grigio with Heirloom Tomatoes and Burrata, *102*, 103

Pinot Noir

    with Brown Sugar Glazed Ham, 190

    with Carrot Ginger Soup with Mint Cashew Pesto, 55

    with Easy Duck Confit with Orange Honey Glaze, 178

    with Roasted Chicken with Fennel and Leek Croutons, 56

    with Rosemary Garlic Pork Loin with Fingerling Potatoes, 35

    with 10-Minute Garlic and Rosemary Roasted Salmon, 92

with White Wine Braised Turkey Legs, 142

pork

    Apple Sausage Stuffing, *140*, 141

    Beer-Braised Carnitas, 82, *83*

    Bratwurst and Cabbage with Dunkel Sauce, *126*, 127

    Rosemary Garlic Pork Loin with Fingerling Potatoes, *34*, 35

Porter-Braised Short Rib Nachos, *150*, 151

potatoes

    Chipotle Roasted Potatoes, *106*, 107

    Roasted Fingerling Potatoes with Caviar and Smoked Salmon, *206*, 207

    Rosemary Garlic Pork Loin with Fingerling Potatoes, *34*, 35

    Slow-Cooker Mashed Potatoes, 128, *129*

Pumpkin Pot de Crème with Maple Bourbon Whipped Cream, *144*, 145

Pumpkin Seed Brittle, 182, *183*

Q

Quick-Pickled Onions, 78, *79*

r

Red Wine Braised Leg of Lamb, 166, *167*

Rhone wine blends with Mushroom and Pancetta Tart, 174, *175*

rice beer with Apricot Curry Chicken Sandwiches, *46, 47*

Riesling with White Wine Braised Turkey Legs, 142

Risotto, Make-Ahead Parmesan, *168,* 169

Roasted Cauliflower and Pomegranate Farro, *180,* 181

Roasted Chicken with Fennel and Leek Croutons, 56, *57*

Roasted Fingerling Potatoes with Caviar and Smoked Salmon, *206,* 207

Rosé with Easy Duck Confit with Orange Honey Glaze, 178, *179*

Rosemary Garlic Pork Loin with Fingerling Potatoes, *34,* 35

s

Saison ale

with Seafood Boil, 68

with White Wine Braised Turkey Legs, 142, *143*

salads

Butternut Squash Salad with Roasted Shallot Dressing, *164,* 165

Fava Bean and Cucumber Salad, 44, *45*

Orange and Olive Salad, *176, 177*

Shaved Asparagus Salad, 32, *33*

Shredded Kale and Brussels Sprouts Salad, 138, *139*

salsas

Pineapple-Avocado Salsa, 104, *105*

Tomatillo and Avocado Salsa, *80,* 81

Salmon, 10-Minute Garlic and Rosemary Roasted, 92, *93*

Sancerre

with Chilled Shrimp with Cilantro Crème Fraîche, *42, 43*

with Dried Cherry and Sage Goat Cheese, *136,* 137

with Herbed Feta Dip, 28

sangria with Porter-Braised Short Rib Nachos, *150,* 151

Sautéed Green Beans with Miso-Mustard Vinaigrette, *94,* 95

Sauvignon Blanc

with Chilled Shrimp with Cilantro Crème Fraîche, *42, 43*

with Asparagus, Green Onion, and Feta Frittata, 22

with Orange and Olive Salad, *176,* 177

seafood

Coconut Curry Mussels, 52, *53*

Chilled Shrimp with Cilantro Crème Fraîche, *42, 43*

Lobster Relish, with Gazpacho, *90,* 91

10-Minute Garlic and Rosemary Roasted Salmon, 92, *93*

Seafood Boil recipes

Fennel Bread, *66, 67*

IPA Quick-Pickle Green Beans, *64, 65*

Seafood Boil, 68, *69*

Sorbet and Prosecco, *70,* 71

Shaved Asparagus Salad, 32, *33*

sherry, with Chorizo Gougéres, 88, *89*

Short Ribs, Porter-Braised, Nachos, *150,* 151

Shredded Kale and Brussels Sprouts Salad, 138, *139*

Shrimp, Chilled, with Cilantro Crème Fraîche, *42, 43*

slaw, pickled, 47

Slow-Cooker Mashed Potatoes, 128, *129*

Smoked Paprika and Maple Carrots, 194, *195*

Smoked Sea Salt Mescal Margaritas, 74, *75*

Sorbet and Prosecco, *70,* 71

soups

Carrot Ginger Soup with Mint Cashew Pesto, *54,* 55

Gazpacho with Lobster Relish, *90,* 91

Spanish Garnacha with White Wine Braised Turkey Legs, 142, *143*

Spanish rosé, with Gazpacho with Lobster Relish, *90,* 91

Speck and Mozzarella Crostini with Truffle Oil, 124, *125*

Sriracha Mayonnaise, 47

Strawberries, Black Pepper–Balsamic, *20,* 21

Summer Soirée recipes

    Chorizo Gougéres, 88, *89*

    Gazpacho with Lobster Relish, *90,* 91

    Sautéed Green Beans with Miso-Mustard Vinaigrette, *94,* 95

    10-Minute Garlic and Rosemary Roasted Salmon, 92, *93*

    Vanilla Bean and Bourbon Peaches, 96, *97*

Syrah

    with Grilled Flat Iron with Pineapple-Avocado Salsa, 104

    with Mushroom and Pancetta Tart, 174, *175*

t

10-Minute Garlic and Rosemary Roasted Salmon, 92, *93*

Thanksgiving with Friends recipes

    Apple and Sausage Stuffing, *140,* 141

    Bourbon Amaretto Cooler, 134, *135*

Dried Cherry and Sage Goat Cheese, *136,* 137

Pumpkin Pot de Crème with Maple Bourbon Whipped Cream, *144, 145*

Shredded Kale and Brussels Sprouts Salad, 138, *139*

White Wine Braised Turkey Legs, 142, *143*

Thyme-Honey Syrup, 40

Tomatillo and Avocado Salsa, *80,* 81

Torrontes with Blistered Shishito Peppers with Sea Salt and Fish Sauce, 100–101

Tuscan blends, with Red Wine Braised Leg of Lamb, 166, *167*

V

Vanilla Bean and Bourbon Peaches, 96, *97*

Vanilla Panna Cotta with Blackstrap Molasses and Graham Crackers, 130, *131*

vegetables

    Asparagus, Green Onion and Feta Frittata, 22, *23*

    Shaved Asparagus Salad, 32, *33*

    Blistered Shishito Peppers with Sea Salt and Fish Sauce, 100

    Brussels Sprouts Salad, with Shredded Kale, 138, *139*

    Burrata, and Heirloom Tomatoes, *102,* 103

Butternut Squash Salad with Roasted Shallot Dressing, *164,* 165

Chipotle Roasted Potatoes, *106,* 107

Creamed Parmesan Collard Greens, *192,* 193

Heirloom Tomatoes and Burrata, *102,* 103

IPA Quick-Pickle Green Beans, 64, *65*

Roasted Cauliflower and Pomegranate Farro, *180,* 181

Roasted Fingerling Potatoes with Caviar and Smoked Salmon, *206,* 207

Rosemary Garlic Pork Loin with Fingerling Potatoes, *34,* 35

Sautéed Green Beans with Miso-Mustard Vinaigrette, *94,* 95

Shaved Asparagus Salad, 32, *33*

Shredded Kale and Brussels Sprouts Salad, 138, *139*

Slow-Cooker Mashed Potatoes, 128, *129*

Smoked Paprika and Maple Carrots, 194, *195*

Verdicchio, 22

    with Orange and Olive Salad, 177

vinaigrette, 44, 95

W

whisky

    Bourbon Amaretto Cooler, 134, *135*

    Bourbon Pecan Pie Shortbread

    Maple Bourbon Whipped Cream, 145

    Whisky Caramel Brownies, 156, *156*

    Vanilla Bean and Bourbon Peaches, 96, *97*

Whisky Caramel Brownies, 156, *156*

White Wine Braised Turkey Legs, 142, *143*

Wine and Dine recipes

    Bacon-Wrapped Dates with Rosemary Goat Cheese, 162, *162*

    Blue Cheese and Honey, 170, *171*

    Butternut Squash Salad with Roasted Shallot Dressing, *164,* 165

    Make-Ahead Parmesan Risotto, *168,* 169

    Red Wine Braised Leg of Lamb, 166, *167*

wines. *See individual names*

Winter Harvest recipes

    Easy Duck Confit with Orange Honey Glaze, 178, *179*

    Mushroom and Pancetta Tart, 174, *175*

    Orange and Olive Salad, *176,* 177

    Pumpkin Seed Brittle, 182, *183*

    Roasted Cauliflower and Pomegranate Farro, *180,* 181

Winter Pimm's Punch, 186, *187*

witbier with Apricot Curry Chicken Sandwiches, *46, 47*

Wraps, Jamón Serrano Manchego, with Quince Paste, 18, *19*

Z

Zinfandel

    with Beer-Braised Carnitas, 82, *83*

    with Porter-Braised Short Rib Nachos, *150,* 151